A SPIRITUALITY
FOR THE LONG HAUL

A SPIRITUALITY
FOR THE LONG HAUL

Biblical Risk and Moral Stand

ROBERT S. BILHEIMER

FORTRESS PRESS   PHILADELPHIA

Biblical quotations, unless otherwise noted, are from the Revised Standard Version of the Bible, copyright 1946, 1952, © 1971, 1973 by the Division of Christian Education of the National Council of the Churches of Christ in the U.S.A. and are used by permission.

COPYRIGHT © 1984 BY FORTRESS PRESS

Library of Congress Cataloging in Publication Data

Bilheimer, Robert S., 1917–
    A spirituality for the long haul.

    Includes bibliographical references.
    ✓1. Spiritual life—Biblical teaching. I. Title.
BS680.S7B54   1984   248.4   83–48918
ISBN 0–8006–1760–6

K465J83   Printed in the United States of America   1–1760

FOR DOROTHY
who exhibits what this book describes

Contents

Acknowledgments   ix

Part I
THE AXIS OF BIBLICAL SPIRITUALITY   1

1. Christian Spirituality: Difference and Coherence   5
2. God's Graciousness: Mystery and Clarity   11
3. The Human Condition   18

Part II
PEOPLE AND PEOPLES   25

4. Peoples: The Matrix of Human Identity   29
5. Peoples: Creativity and Character   37
6. People and Person   44
7. The Beginning of Spirituality: Peoplehood as a
   Boundary of the Human Spirit   50
8. The Content of Spirituality: Identity in Christ   55
9. The Enduring Problem and Strength of Christian
   Spirituality   64

Part III
SPIRITUALITY AMID THE LOST   71

10. Sin: A Compulsion in the Mask of Freedom   75
11. Powers: Domination in the Guise of Empowerment 86
12. Creature: Dependence in the Cloak of Autonomy   92
13. Lost: The Meeting Point of God and the Human
    Spirit   98
14. Crossing the Boundary: Deep Calls to Deep   107
15. The Always-New World of Spirituality in Christ 115

Part IV
SPIRITUALITY: BEING AND DOING, UNITED   125

16. Mission to Peoples with Concern for Persons   129
17. Mission to Persons in Awareness of Peoplehood   140

A Concluding Note   153

Notes   154

Acknowledgements

The reader will discover in the following pages most of the people to whom I am indebted in writing this book. I am grateful to them and appreciate the personal experience with which many of them were associated. In addition, my wife, to whom the book is dedicated, and three sons—Bob, Rick, and Rog—provided the vitality of family discussion and criticism. As the book was being formulated, successive groups of Fellows of the Institute for Ecumenical and Cultural Research, Collegeville, Minnesota, aided me by comment both direct and indirect. An interdisciplinary group of faculty at St. Cloud State University, the "Lunch Bunch," listened patiently, questioned, and reacted helpfully in a series of discussions over two years. The following read all or parts of the manuscript and offered comment, frequently in detail and always of value: Roy M. Anker, Cynthia Bourgeault, Joan Chittister, Daniel Durken, Paul Harrison, Patrick Henry, William L. Lane, Theodore Runyon, Samuel Terrien, to whom I owe the subtitle, and Robert VanDale. I am of course responsible for the result, but the responsibility is lighter because of their help. I thank them heartily together with Dolores Schuh, who typed the final manuscript.

Robert S. Bilheimer

Collegeville, Minnesota
Thanksgiving 1982

Part I

THE AXIS OF
BIBLICAL SPIRITUALITY

All meanings of "axis" have two elements in common. One element is a line or structure related to two poles; the other is either a motion that turns around the line or a form organized in reference to the line.

Biblical spirituality grows out of the axis between God and humanity, turns around it, and from it derives motion and shape. In the many varieties of Christian spirituality, the common element is the power of its axis.

Scripture illumines this in its own ways. Primary attention falls upon the graciousness of God, one pole of the axis, and upon the condition of human beings, the other pole. Each pole has its own structure. Spirituality comes to life when the structure of the divine pole of the axis connects with the structure of its human terminus.

Part I begins (chapter 1) with two examples of variety in Christian spirituality and points to the coherence in this variety. Attention then turns in chapter 2 to God and the structure of the divine pole of the axis. Chapter 3 is concerned with the general characteristics of the human pole of the axis of spirituality.

1

Christian Spirituality: Difference and Coherence

In October 1974, I called upon my friend Thomas Stransky, a Paulist father, at the Paulist headquarters in Scarsdale, New York. We had met in the ecumenical movement—Father Stransky from the Roman Catholic side, I from the Protestant. On this occasion we were concerned with the spiritual climate of the time, which was marked by a myriad of tendencies: the promise upon payment of considerable money, of quick development of individual human potential; the concept that divine salvation can be instantly grasped; spiritual guarantees of inner peace, economic prosperity, and physical health; disillusionment with the institutions of society and their processes, especially the political ones; a trend towards hedonism; and hesitancy in the churches to act. Despite this, we noted that many people, both secular and religious, had their eyes fixed on a high quality of spiritual and ethical life for themselves and for their society. We were not in a doomsday mood, but a sober one, because the problems were serious. A pause occurred in our conversation. Stransky broke it. "What we need," he said, "is a spirituality for the long haul."

That stopped conversation and provoked thought. If my friend had said, "We need the right kind of spirituality," he would have implied something that was in contrast to a wrong kind of spirituality, possibly a spirituality in a narrower sense, encompassing only prayer and contemplation. "For the long haul" seemed to include this important aspect of spirituality, but also to imply something more. But what? Curiously, I did not ask. The more I thought, however, the more a "spirituality for the long haul" seemed to involve a way of life, a thrust

5

of purpose, commitment, and character through the years. This suggests that everyone has a spirituality of some sort, whether for the short run or the long haul, whether responsive to a court of high appeal or to no court at all. The implication is that a person's spirituality results from a decision made somewhere and somehow along the line concerning the questions: What kind of a person do I wish to be? What do I want to do with my life? To whom or to what do I intend to be loyal? In what community am I most at home?

This book discusses spirituality in the broad sense reflected in these questions, and we look to Scripture for help in answering them. I turn to Scripture for many reasons, for example, because of the impact of long ecumenical experience upon me. Living and working with people of different races, nationalities, cultures, and church traditions makes one realize that one's own culture and tradition are decidedly one among many. My own American background as a white, middle-class, Presbyterian male became vividly relative to others when placed in an international, interdenominational, intercultural, and interracial setting of men and women. Such experience does not require denial of one's own background, even if that were possible, but it does require listening to and appreciating others. In a word, ecumenical experience has the effect of making all traditions, including one's own, relative to others.

Ecumenical experience drove me to the roots of my own tradition. It forced me to read further in American history in an endeavor to understand my own place in it; it also made me turn to the Bible, which I had long understood to be the norm and source of Christian faith. In this I was supported by ecumenical church experience, where I found that people from all church traditions recognize Scripture to be in some sense the norm of faith. There is no agreement upon what that sense is, but when they confront one another and when they confront the modern world, all traditions turn ultimately to Scripture. The ecumenical age has not led away from the Bible but to it.

If that is true of church traditions, it is also true of spirituality. We Christians differ in our conceptions of Christian living. At the same time there are some things we hold in common. Christian spirituality expresses both difference and coherence. Consider, for instance, the spiritualities of two important although little-known people.

He opened the book and found the place where it was written,
"The Spirit of the Lord is upon me,
because he has anointed me to preach good news to the poor.
He has sent me to proclaim release to the captives
and recovering of sight to the blind,
to set at liberty those who are oppressed,
to proclaim the acceptable year of the Lord." (Luke 4:17–19)

In the spring of 1964 our four-seater plane, en route from Salisbury to Kitwe, dipped low over the place where the secretary-general of the United Nations, Dag Hammarskjöld, had recently crashed and died. Hammarskjöld once wrote that "God desires our independence."[1] That was an appropriate word for us in the small plane. We were on our way to meet with a company of Blacks and Whites concerned with justice in the white-dominated areas of southern Africa.

At Kitwe Z. K. Matthews spoke on behalf of the vast black population of South Africa. He had a right to do so. A man of uncommon abilities and international reputation, Matthews embodied another of Hammarskjöld's notes: "In our era, the road to holiness necessarily passes through the world of action."[2] Matthews had spent his life teaching young Blacks, appealing to the government and pleading the cause of black justice abroad. As a close colleague of Nobel Peace laureate Albert Luthuli, Matthews had been a leader of the African National Congress, one of the African organizations which white South Africans feared most.

Matthews said that in South Africa the "history of relations between Black and White ever since they met on the banks of the Fish River in the Cape in the eighteenth century had been one of conflict." Until 1906, Blacks had used every weapon at their disposal to defend themselves against white invasion and encroachment. After the Zulu War of that year Blacks had changed; they sought to enter white civilization and to achieve dignity in the midst of misery by reason and persuasion. For half a century and more, however, appeals for a reasonable approach to the problems of the country had been met by constant hardening of the white heart, so that ruthless imprisonment awaited all Blacks who actively opposed white policy. Matthews concluded his review with a question: "When the flower of African youth are being sentenced to long terms of imprisonment during peace time for fight-

ing for their legitimate rights in what they believe to be the only ways
open to them, can we say that the Christian thing to do is to advise
them to acquiesce in their present situation and wait, Micawber-like,
for something to turn up?" Matthews never simply waited. He spent
his life proclaiming release to the captives and seeking their freedom.

The spirituality of justice takes two forms, one violent, the other
nonviolent. Both forms are expressed in the Bible, and Z. K. Matthews
felt the appeal of both. For nearly all of his life Matthews believed that
following Jesus required nonviolence when dealing with injustice.
Matthews's address at Kitwe however, delivered near the end of his
life, was entitled "The End of Nonviolence?" and reflected the tension
between the spirituality of nonviolence and the spirituality of the holy
war. ("So perish all thine enemies, O Lord! But thy friends be like the
sun as he rises in his might" [Judg. 5:31].) Matthews had neither joy
nor sense of triumph when considering armed conflict. He was driven
to it by desperation in order to fulfill his commitment "to set at liberty
those who are oppressed."

> Likewise the Spirit helps us in our weakness; for we do not know how to
> pray as we ought, but the Spirit himself intercedes for us with sighs too
> deep for words. And he who searches the hearts of men knows what is the
> mind of the Spirit, because the Spirit intercedes for the saints according to
> the will of God. (Rom. 8:26–27)

Claire Hahn Becker, a striking woman at the height of her
capacities, entered the room where a dozen people were already
gathered. They had come to reflect upon their faith in God. Since they
were strangers to one another, it was necessary for each to speak
autobiographically at first. Claire had this to say about herself: "I was a
nun, having entered the convent at age sixteen, but leaving prior to the
sixties because I discovered that I professed a faith I had never tested.
Since 1962 I have taught English at Fordham University. When
students knew that I was formerly a nun, they came ostensibly to talk
about term papers but really to ask why I had left, whether I hated God
now, and what faith meant. I suddenly had an apostolate among the
students. Yet I did not have time to think or talk to God, that is, to talk it
all out. I was also a bit angry. Therefore I did not respond to the
students' questions really, but listened.

"Last year, I found that I have terminal cancer, with only a year to live. I am now in remission, and I do not know how many years I have left. I was very angry at the God who would torture a person this way. I saw intense suffering in the hospital. A woman with a double amputation screamed terribly when they changed her bandages. The nurse said to her, 'Put your faith in the Lord,' and the woman replied, 'When you do that, you get hit.' She then asked me, 'Do you have faith in the Lord?' 'Well, yes,' I replied. 'So do I,' she said, and then asked, 'But do you like him?' 'No,' I confessed, 'I do not like the Lord.' 'I don't either,' she said. 'God's not our kind of folks.' "

I did not see Claire Becker for eighteen months. When I next saw her the remission was over, and we met the day after she had been released from the hospital following another in a series of operations. In a long conversation with her and her husband, I discovered again the utter openness with which she talked of her situation. In due course I said, "Claire, it seems to me that the Devil has won a battle, but we both believe he does not win the war." "Not so," she quickly replied, "everything is from God and is good." "But," I returned, "I feel somehow guilty here with you. I have my work, which is exciting; a family that is fine, thriving, and intact; a home in the beautiful woods. It is not right to have all of this and for you to be in your situation." "You are wrong," she said. "Accept what you have and give thanks; you never know what God has in store for you."

Eight months later Claire died. The card that announced her death only had on it these lines from W. B. Yeats:

So great a sweetness flows into the breast
We must laugh and we must sing,
We are blest by everything,
Everything we look upon is blest.[3]

How shall we live our lives? Z. K. Matthews found in Scripture a clear warrant for struggling against oppression; Claire Hahn Becker found resources for meeting life's doubts and sufferings. Scripture also contains warrants for other spiritualities. Scripture gives reason to adopt a spirituality of obedience to the law, whether the law of Moses or the new law of Christ. The spirituality of the priest, the lonely calling of the prophet, and the reassuring guidance of the lover of wisdom all stand side by side in Scripture. The inwardness of prayer and praise, the surrender of self, the agonies of struggle, and the power of spiritual transformation are also present. Hope, which implies a spirituality of future expectation, overarches all. One need not look far to discover strands in Scripture that define varied spiritual attitudes and styles.

It is possible to respond to these many types of biblical spirituality by picking and choosing among them. That is probably inevitable. Passages that speak to my need, and thus become favorite passages, will be different from those that appeal to my closest friend—or to myself at a different time in life. Some passages lift the spirit because of their sheer beauty, and others lie close because of earlier associations. It is all but inescapable that some passages appeal and others remain remote.

Nevertheless, this natural tendency can lead to the construction of a private, self-justifying Bible composed only of pleasing parts drawn from the whole. If my spirituality is drawn chiefly from a few passages of my own choosing, I short change myself. If my own needs and, even more, my own view of my own needs determine which portion of Scripture is most gratifying, I slip into a spirituality of personal preference, molding God to my own desires. Z. K. Matthews might have quickly seized a gun, certain that God was on his side, yet he did not do that, although he modified his views about the efficacy of nonviolence. Claire Becker might have tried to flee from doubts and to deny her cancer by taking false refuge in the Spirit, but she did not do that, although early death filled her with sorrow. Both refused to pick and choose and thus take the road of private preference. For them, spirituality rose higher.

Claire Becker and Z. K. Matthews never met. Matthews's life spanned the first seventy and more years of this century, Becker's some forty-five years at mid-century. Matthews was black, South African, male, Protestant, cultured, and much traveled. Becker was white, American, female, Catholic, cultured, and little traveled. Matthews was concerned with gross injustice, Becker with erosion at the foundation of life. Though life had placed and nurtured them in two different worlds, they would—had they met—have recognized themselves in one another. They would have discovered that each expressed the coherence and meaning of biblical spirituality. Amid lostness, they found themselves by means of graciousness.

2

God's Graciousness: Mystery and Clarity

In biblical spirituality, God is primary. Everything proceeds from Scripture's awareness and knowledge of God. The direction is not the other way—from feelings, thoughts, and experience "up" to God. God is first. The Divine Presence makes itself known. That happens in a particular way, and when it happens, God's graciousness exhibits a structure of its own.

The way by which God's presence becomes known may be seen in Israel's memory of how God dealt with its people. The event that constituted and nourished Israel as God's people is recorded in these words:

> " 'A wandering Aramean was my father; and he went down into Egypt and sojourned there, few in number; and there he became a nation, great, mighty and populous. And the Egyptians treated us harshly, and afflicted us, and laid upon us hard bondage. Then we cried to the Lord the God of our fathers, and the Lord heard our voice, and saw our affliction, our toil, and our oppression; and the Lord brought us out of Egypt with a mighty hand and an outstretched arm, with great terror, with signs and wonders; and he brought us into this place and gave us this land, a land flowing with milk and honey.' " (Deut. 26:5–9; see also Deut. 6:20–25; Josh. 24:2–13)

This passage, which is of great antiquity, affirms God's graciousness. "We cried . . . the Lord heard . . . saw . . . and brought." That is graciousness. It signifies not only that God exists, not only that God is present, but also that God listens and responds to the afflicted human cry. This graciousness did not become evident through speculation or abstract reasoning but through the specific situation of a people, made desperate by oppression, being given a place in the purpose of God. God's graciousness is known in a particular human situation, but not merely momentarily.

When one considers it, this passage is curious, even peculiar. It speaks of God, but scarcely says who God is. There is no attention to even modest theological precision. Moreover, the passage refers to a historical situation, but without what either ancient historians, like Thucydides, or modern historians would call decent history writing: few facts, trends, personalities, causes, and effects are mentioned. It records neither abstract faith nor cold history.

The passage, like Scripture as a whole in its different modes, is a confession of faith with history at its center. Used in liturgy, this account focused the people's attention upon the action of God at the decisive moment of their past, even as they worshiped in the present.[1] That is the way it is throughout Scripture. Memory preserved the power of the originating event in Egypt; worship and life validated the memory again and again over centuries; and new events gathered the whole in further interpretation. These new events included the moments—as the Exodus event included Moses' encounter with God—when God's Word was directly communicated, and they included events in Israel's history. The result was the interpretation and the reinterpretation of the original. By such means God's graciousness became known.

This method also communicates something about God's graciousness itself. Graciousness is not a general diffusion from an overflowing cosmic source, resulting in a warm spiritual bath. On the contrary, divine graciousness has its own structure, one that unites clarity and mystery.

From the beginning the people and writers of Scripture knew that God's actions had unmistakable, even overpowering clarity. The biblical story includes accounts of people's hesitation, struggle, doubt, and disbelief. These accounts, however, do not register confusion about God so much as a disarming honesty. The Bible is not a neat fairy tale; it takes human qualities and problems seriously. Within these human realities, the clarity of God's purpose stands forth, yet not alone.

Behind the moments of even the greatest clarity, the unfathomable inspires reverence, awe, fear, and sometimes a nearly absurd familiarity, even as it is always known to be gracious.

Moses said, "I pray thee, show me thy glory." And he said, "I will make all my goodness pass before you, and will proclaim before you my name 'The Lord'; and I will be gracious to whom I will be gracious, and will show mercy on whom I will show mercy. But," he said, "you cannot see my face; for man shall not see me and live." And the Lord said, "Behold, there is a place by me where you shall stand upon the rock; and while my glory passes by I will put you in a cleft of the rock, and I will cover you with my hand until I have passed by; then I will take away my hand, and you shall see my back; but my face shall not be seen." (Exod. 33:18–23)

By this account no mystic vision of the One comes first, to be followed by a clear application of its meaning. Here, as elsewhere in Scripture, the movement goes the other way. Speech is heard, its source hidden. For Moses, as for Abraham before him and the prophets after him, God is heard and not seen, even if on occasion there are visible elements in the great visitations. One reads in virtually every portion of Scripture about the name of God, the Lord, and one finds a strain of reference to the glory of God. Yet neither the strong belief in the power of the name, which suggests that God is heard, nor the perceptions of God's glory, which suggest that something of the divine is seen, remove the ultimate mystery of God.

Likewise, Scripture does not have interest in, does not speculate about, or lay claim to direct knowledge of what philosophers and much of church doctrine speak of as the "being" of God. That tradition is largely Greek in origin, which contrasts with the Hebrew outlook. Samuel Terrien writes: "Quite differently, the Hebraic expression *da'at Elohim,* 'knowledge of God,' points to a reality which at once includes and transcends intellectual disquisition. It designates the involvement of man's total personality in the presence of Yahweh through the prophetic word, the cultic celebration, and the psychological mode of communion in faith. In the Hebraic sense of 'knowledge of God,' theology does not mean an objective science of divine things. Although it uses the critical faculties of the mind, it proceeds both from an inner commitment to a faith and from a participation in the destiny of a people."[2]

Behind this commitment and participation lies the mystery which produces clarity. The passage which says "You cannot see my face" is clear-cut in tone and content. So, overall, is the Hebrew knowledge of God. In the originating and continuing experiences of God's graciousness, mystery and clarity are both present.

This extraordinary union is evident also when the perspective shifts from the people's history to the intimate moments of praise, thanksgiving, and communion. The Psalms constituted the prayer book of the people, and from its wealth none has more power than Psalm 103:

> Bless the Lord, O my soul;
> and all that is within me, bless his holy name!
> Bless the Lord, O my soul
>   and forget not all his benefits,
> who forgives all your iniquity,
>   who heals all your diseases,
> who redeems your life from the Pit,
>   who crowns you with steadfast love and mercy,
> who satisfies you with good as long as you live
>   so that your youth is renewed like the eagle's. (vv. 1–5)

Further lines of the psalm are set within the memory: "He made known his ways to Moses, his acts to the people of Israel" (v. 7). The psalm praises, gives thanks for, and expresses communion with God's love and forgiveness: "For as the heavens are high above the earth, so great is his steadfast love toward those who fear him; as far as the east is from the west, so far does he remove our transgressions from us" (vv. 11–12). In praise and thanks this poetry confesses an ultimate knowledge: "His kingdom rules over all. . . . Bless the Lord, all his works, in all places of his dominion. Bless the Lord, O my soul" (vv. 19, 22).

Psalm 103 refers to many of the great theological problems that confront human reason: the problem of evil, God's relation to the realms of nature and history, the issue of law and grace, the qualities of love and forgiveness, despair and hope, justice and oppression, death and destiny. The knowledge of God contained in these words does not avoid such problems but goes through and beyond them. Nowhere do the terms "mystery" and "clarity" appear. The act of inner communion, however, embraces them.

One evening, when I was pastor of a downtown church, the phone rang. I was informed that a close friend, one of my chief advisors in the church, had died unexpectedly of a heart attack earlier in the evening, at his modest summer cottage. At the moment of the phone call his wife was en route back to their home in town. I met her on the front lawn. Dry-eyed, she looked at me with pain, saying with a wistful smile that will not fade from memory: "So much is left unsaid." Neither she nor her husband were reticent persons; they had been married over thirty years. In a single sentence she had spoken of the person she knew and still did not know, of the veil that remains after a life's revelation of the other. In a word she had expressed the paradox of knowing through not knowing. The anguished sentence spoke of clarity united with mystery.

After this fashion, from Abraham to Moses and the prophets, from the Exodus to the settlement in Canaan and the development of Israel's tradition, from the sacred places to the Temple, from the literature of wisdom to the poetry of the Psalms, from Job to the apocalyptic expectations, the formulators of the Old Testament traditions perceived God's graciousness. They understood the unfathomable because of God's unmistakable ways with them. Receiving a promise, experiencing a deliverance, hearing a command, the biblical writers knew the meaning of "the Lord," the name given by God, which God himself spoke. Knowing divine mercy, they did not hesitate to testify that the Holy One is merciful; experiencing salvation, they confessed that God is Savior as well as Creator; conscious of being judged and overruled by God, they perceived that God is judge; recognizing that love comes from God, they acknowledged that God is love. These and other descriptions, however, flow from the mystery of God and lead back into it. They do not penetrate or remove it; Scripture's knowledge of God has a different effect. Scripture discloses the clarity with which the "self-concealing" God addresses humanity.

The structure of God's graciousness does not change as Scripture moves from the Old to the New Testament. Yahweh, the Lord, is the One whom Jesus called Father. Graciousness appears in the New Testament with the definitive brilliance of light in darkness. Jesus Christ increases the mystery and clarity of God to the point where each becomes absolute. Hitherto the graciousness of God had been known in the speech of God. Now it is acted out in the flesh, a mystery so impenetrable that it has been a stumbling block and foolishness both to those of ancient times and to those of the present. Peter, James, and John did not comprehend the meaning of the altered countenance and the glistening garments white as light (Matt. 17:1-8; Mark 9:2-10; Luke 9:28-36). The Divine Presence did not appear to sight but, as in occasions gone by, spoke from within the depths of a cloud. The mystery of God hidden is not removed but compounded by the mystery of God speaking: "This is my Son, my chosen; listen to him." Yet the action of God-in-Christ was of a particular kind. Each of the first three gospels reports that after the transfiguring act, Jesus went at once to "the street," among the crowds to heal. This act and its consequence exhibit the clarity of a human life conformed to God's will. Whether the transfiguration of the carpenter's son strikes one through speech, act, or relationships—or all of these together—it is like dazzling clothing, visible but yet beyond vision. Noticeably this life of Christ never stands by itself, nor does it draw attention to itself alone. It is not autonomous. Christ is the singular speech of God addressed to humanity to serve God's purpose for humanity. Taken as a whole or in any particular, this Word in the flesh enhances the mystery and sharpens the clarity of God's graciousness. "For it is the God who said, 'Let light shine out of darkness,' who has shone in our hearts to give the light of the knowledge of the glory of God in the face of Christ" (2 Cor. 4:6).

The union of mystery and clarity in God's graciousness has direct consequence for spirituality. Both are needed. Especially during this time, when the world's change and turmoil crowd in upon us, it is a consolation to know of God's mystery, of the existence of something unknown, of God being different from our pain, cruelty, and confusion. We need to take refuge in the Unknowable One. We can understand why, with the hope and much of the substance of Israel's faith seemingly shattered by the Babylonian Empire, Isaiah of the exile had reason to write:

> For my thoughts are not your thoughts,
>   neither are your ways my ways, says the Lord.
> For as the heavens are higher than the earth,
>   so are my ways higher than your ways
>   and my thoughts than your thoughts. (Isa. 55:8–9)

Nevertheless, mystery may also lose its meaning. If there is only a sense of the unknown about God, where shall one turn when God appears to be absent and when, in prayer, one speaks to a seeming void? Or, when one is driven to take refuge in the Unknowable One, is it not possible to delight too much in mystery, forgetting purpose and action?

Clarity is needed in union with mystery. The prophet of the exile followed the previous words with others:

"For as the rain and the snow come from heaven,
  and return not thither but water the earth,
making it bring forth and sprout,
  giving seed to the sower and bread to the eater,
so shall my word be that goes forth from my mouth;
  it shall not return to me empty,
but it shall accomplish that which I purpose,
  and prosper in the thing for which I sent it." (Isa. 55:10–11)

The Word "goes forth." The ways that are not our ways are clear and crystalline, but not sterile: the Word "shall accomplish."

As the mystery of God can lose its meaning, so the clarity of God's Word—even though it be the sinew of our spiritual flesh—can be dissipated. Two familiar tendencies illustrate the point. The first concerns the use of words to express the verities of faith. Words should lead beyond themselves, as icons which open vistas and give access to the sacred Word. Instead, words frequently lose their power to lead. They remain inert, correctly used yet powerless, idols which, because they open no vistas, function only to contain and control the sacred.[3] Perhaps nothing expresses this more than usage of the sentence "Christ died for our sins" or its equivalent. Too often repeated, frequently in the same church service, it becomes an idol, closing out mystery and dissipating clarity. Is that not true also of "Jesus," of "love," of "peace," and of other great words in our spiritual vocabulary?

The tendency to distort God's Word also reduces its clarity. "Let justice roll down like waters, and righteousness like an everflowing stream" wrote the prophet Amos (5:24). Not infrequently the clarity of these words becomes a cover for the reformer's own ideas so that justice is reduced to less than God's intent. Today the complexity of society and the fascination of moderns with it reduce God's justice to but one among many elements of the decision-making process, obscuring the power of the demand. Thus the clarity of God's graciousness becomes enmeshed, losing its power to illumine.

To take refuge in mystery may lead to a spirituality of escape; undue preoccupation with what is clear may lead to distortion. Mystery requires clarity lest mystery evaporate; clarity requires mystery lest clarity be corrupted. A spirituality truly drawn from Scripture unites the mystery and clarity inherent in God's graciousness.

3

The Human Condition

Biblical spirituality demands knowledge of oneself. Those to whom the Word of the Lord was spoken, those who were drawn into the mystery of God and who perceived the clarity of God, were given a broad but nevertheless particular understanding of themselves. As the great visitation of God came upon Isaiah, he heard "Holy, holy, holy is the Lord of hosts; the whole earth is full of his glory," and the foundations shook. Immediately self-recognition took place: "Woe is me! For I am lost; for I am a man of unclean lips, and I dwell in the midst of a people of unclean lips" (Isa. 6:3–5). That spontaneous, anguished cry was integral to the experience; the uncleanness mattered in the presence of the Holy One. Moreover, Isaiah's understanding of himself was not autonomous, not an independently conceived opinion of his spiritual state. Isaiah's sense of being lost and unclean and his awareness of the uncleanness of his people arose from the presence of the holy. For the remainder of his life as a spokesman of God, Isaiah's intense spirituality consisted of the combination of God's presence and the self-awareness which that presence brings about. Both were necessary.

Scripture is vibrant with the combination of graciousness and self-awareness. The writers of Scripture evaluated the life of the ancient people of Israel and the new people of Christ from the perspective of God's graciousness. This occurred within a vast range of human experience: in slavery, freedom, exile, and occupation; as tribes, a confederacy, a unified nation, and a divided nation; in prosperity and splendor and also in poverty; in decay, discouragement, and despair as well as in creativity, purpose, and hope. This diverse experience was never treated as a mere history of the people but was remembered and interpreted from the perspective of the question: What does God's graciousness mean for us, for our people, and our history? The unfolding answer to that question produced increasing self-knowledge. From the primary viewpoint of God's presence, the biblical writers reinterpreted the character of human life and history.

That viewpoint provided the principle of coherence. Coherence was not achieved by applying principles of philosophy, psychology, social relations, or politics to Israel's life. Moreover, Scripture does not establish coherence through a systematic account of Israel's development, comparing it with other civilizations and then concluding the differences and similarities. Biblical people knew themselves because they understood God's ways with them. A paradox sprang to life: knowledge of God yielded knowledge of self. We moderns go at it in a different way. For us knowledge of the self begins with observation by means of the liberal and the fine arts, the sciences, and our own introspection. Scripture, however, maintains a different order: from God to the self. Because biblical people knew God, they knew the self. That was their principle of coherence. From the knowledge of God all else flowed.

A demand lies implicit in this principle of coherence. Because God's graciousness causes attention to the self, it also requires attention to one's character and to the conditions of life. One might think, for instance, that it is sufficient to note Isaiah's "uncleanness" as a normal human reaction to the presence of "the Lord, high and lifted up," and to conclude that when the central focus is upon the Holy One, all else will fall into place. Similarly one might recall Paul's familiar sentence "For no other foundation can any one lay than that which is laid, which is Jesus Christ" (1 Cor. 3:11) and remember also the parallel thought that concludes the Sermon on the Mount in Matthew's Gospel: "Every one then who hears these words of mine and does them will be like a wise man who built his house upon the rock" (Matt. 7:24). Concentrating upon these statements, one might be led to think that self-knowledge will take care of itself, and that the holy presence, the foundation, the rock is sufficient.

That, however, was not so for the people of Scripture. They felt the need to comprehend life as it is when God's ways are made known. Whether God's presence was made evident in creativity or in promise, in choosing or in purpose, in judgment or in forgiveness, in Word or in

Word made flesh, biblical people came to recognize themselves as they had not done previously, or they were called to understand again what they had understood previously but had forgotten. God's graciousness required a continual exercise in self-recognition as God's ways became known in differing life situations.

What self-understanding emerges? The remainder of this book is devoted to answering that question. Scripture presents an overall perspective which gives shape to everything else that is said about the condition of human beings. In essence, the biblical perspective views human life as subject to immense pressure exercised by ultimate realities and the choice they inevitably require. One statement concerning this appears in Deuteronomy and another in the Gospel of John:

> "I call heaven and earth to witness against you this day, that I have set before you life and death, blessing and curse; therefore choose life, that you and your descendants may live." (Deut. 30:19)

> In him was life, and the life was the light of men. The light shines in the darkness, and the darkness has not overcome it. . . . and men loved darkness rather than light. (John 1:4–5; 3:19)

In Deuteronomy the alternative of life and death, blessing and curse, is stark, resulting in an explicitly stated choice: "Therefore choose life." This presents Israel's ultimate situation in the presence of God and the revelation of God's will in Torah, with the overtones of meaning for humanity implied. In John's Gospel the accent is directly upon human self-discovery in the presence of God's revelation in Jesus Christ: confronted with the ultimate light of God's presence in him, human beings not only discover that ordinary life is darkness but also that they like the darkness.

It would be wrong to gather from this that life consists of a battle between two principles—life, good, and light on the one side and death, evil, and darkness on the other. The Hebrew mind did not operate in this fashion, nor did the Hebrew experience translate into these dualistic terms. The life choice set forth by Deuteronomy and the astonishing meaning of Christ described in John's Gospel reflect another view, They and the biblical writers as a whole present life according to a different outlook. Their orientation, so unusual even for the people of Israel that they revolted against it and so unwonted for many in the early church that they fell away from it, was life consumed by God to the degree that all else seemed to be death, darkness, and evil. For them only God is good, only God gives life, only in God is there light.

From this passionate certainty that God alone matters comes an urgent concern for those who have fallen away from God or who live without God. They are not left to wander in the darkness amid an opaque generality, hoping vaguely for "the light." Out of concern for human life, Scripture penetrates the darkness of human life. While in the wilderness, Israel occasionally felt that life back in Egypt in slavery or the worship of a false god promised more than their pilgrimage with God. Then, as in period after period, the Word which had brought creation out of chaos was required anew because of the inchoate, deceptive attractiveness of life without God. The objective of this concern for the darkness of life is to enable people to understand the human conditions to which God's graciousness is addressed. God's graciousness, we noted, is not a general spiritual diffusion. God's light and power operate with their own specificity. Scripture enables us to understand that God reaches human beings at certain aspects of human existence and to perceive what these aspects are.

The descriptions of the points at which God touches life do not, of course, appear all together and in one place in the Bible. Rather, they unfold. As they unfold they are progressively validated in experience and in reflection upon experience. They are thus developed with cumulative force, in the sense that the earliest discernment of each of them is not denied but taken into subsequent perceptions. The understanding of them deepens and broadens; what is said in the early biblical history about them is drawn out in later, changed circumstances, especially those in which God's Word is directly communicated until finally it is made evident, not in words but in full display.

In the remainder of this book, we shall explore these aspects of the human condition and what they mean for spirituality. Two comments are needed at this point. One concerns the limitations of life;[1] the other concerns the constant character of these limitations.

The first comment may be introduced by reference to general experience in the formation of Christian spirituality. However it may begin, spirituality in its Christian sense frequently develops and deepens when the internal conditions and the events of life hit us hard and make us feel helpless. Both Claire Hahn Becker and Z. K. Matthews knew suffering. Claire Becker knew what it meant to be speechless when the faith which had given purpose to her life had evaporated and yet students came asking about God, and when, later, at the height of her capacities, cancer named an early date for her death. Z. K. Matthews was held down, threatened, driven from his country. He saw his friends and his people oppressed and endangered because of white policy and practice. Both Becker and Matthews suffered because they directly experienced pain and hurt. They also knew the suffering of frustration. In each case hope and aspiration were thwarted because of limitations over which they had no control. Yet at the same time it happened for them that life opened into an empowering knowledge that the limitations are not final. In their respective ways they both found the wonder of Christian spirituality.

Scripture leads one to perceive the boundaries of life and then to go beyond them. Hearing God's Word to them, the authors of Scripture understood that God's presence breaks through at the points where life itself is undeniably limited. "I have seen the affliction of my people who are in Egypt, and have heard their cry because of their taskmasters; I know their sufferings, and I have come down to deliver them out of the hand of the Egyptians" (Exod. 3:7–8). As the meaning of this event unfolded and was progressively validated by the people's experience with God, "taskmasters" and "sufferings" took on broadened significance. Whether the suffering turned out to be hardness of heart, cruelty, the ravages of foreign powers, or the gathering of principalities that hung Jesus on the cross, the cry of God issued from the pressure of human limit and extremity. "My God, my God, why hast thou forsaken me?" (Matt. 27:46; Mark 15:34) expresses the depth of human limitation in that final moment of Jesus' rejection, a rejection which was prior to the ultimate victory over all limitations. From the cry in Egypt to the cry on the cross, biblical spirituality arises when the limitations of human life are met by the mystery and clarity of God's graciousness.

Then a different kind of limit for human life appears. Isaiah's lament "Woe is me" suggests the spiritual necessity of self-recognition. His "unclean" suggests the limitation. Yet there is no leaving the matter there, no implication that guilt ridden and helpless he must remain bound by his uncleanness. In answer to the divine question, Isaiah responds: "Send me." The limit imposed by his uncleanness is super-seded by a limit of another kind, by a new boundary, by a recognition that the final basis or boundary of life is God. Similarly, Jesus' disciples were not left in despair with only his words of rejection by which to interpret the wonder of his life and the meaning of what he had said during it. A new world became present to them, a world in which, because of him, they were reconciled to God and had the sense of a new life, indeed of a new world and a new creation The crux of biblical spirituality became clear. The darkness and imprisonment within which life labors opened into a new, empowering knowledge that the final limits of life are not those which wring a cry of suffering or of dereliction. The final boundary of life is God, the one limit of all existence that provides freedom.

The second comment necessary at this point concerns human limits. In various ways the Bible offers insight and reflection as to what the limitations to life actually are and how people may recognize their impact and importance for life, including life with God. Stated differ-ently these insights and reflections show the concern of biblical writers with self-recognition at fundamental levels of life. The biblical writers are not, for instance, concerned with pointing out inherent laws or static conditions, exhorting us to conform to them. Similarly, they are not content to describe different human moods, like despair and joy, and to accompany their descriptions with advice as to how these may be handled.[2] Rather, the authors of Scripture, both directly and indirectly, point to aspects of life which are unveiled by their knowledge of God. The cumulative effect is the portrayal of constant conditions of human life in which the limits to life are consistently and forcefully met. This provides a certain type of ordering. In the custom-ary yet highly theological phrase, life ceases to be "one damned thing after another," a bewildering series of unrelated limitations and frus-trations punctuated now and then with brighter moments. The limita-tions which cause suffering have an order about them. They are constant aspects of being human, and because they are such, they provide a means of self-recognition. These constants in the human condition have, in a very broad sense, both sociological and psycholog-ical importance. Supremely, however, their importance is theological. Scripture testifies to the fact that God's graciousness operates at these constant levels of human limitation.

Part II

PEOPLE
AND PEOPLES

If the experience of God, recorded in many biblical accents over a long period of time, produced knowledge of the human condition, what is that knowledge? What self-understanding comes from biblical knowledge of God? If the axis or pole of Christian spirituality fits into the mystery and clarity of God's graciousness at one end, into what does it fit at the other, human end? And what is the result for spirituality?

The six chapters in this section consider scriptural thought concerning peoples and their significance for spirituality. The theme is that ancient Israel's achievement of identity provided an understanding of peoples and peoplehood which forms a core, a base line, the first point for human self-understanding, which is fundamental to human relationship with God.

4

Peoples: The Matrix of Human Identity

One day in March 1957 I met with a group of students in Ludhiana, India. They were intensely nationalistic. At the time I was on the staff of the World Council of Churches, based in Geneva, Switzerland, then the mecca of internationalism. I anticipated that I would be received as an international and that the tough issues could be discussed within the objective reasonableness of an internationalistic atmosphere. It was not so. The students cared not a whit whom I represented; to them I was an American. Their anger at the United States, its foreign policy, and specifically, its treatment of India was acute, and their language shrill.

After a short time I became aware that something was happening to me. I also had been critical of U.S. foreign policy, at times almost as vociferously as the Indian students. Yet neither my internationalism nor my attitude toward U.S. policy helped. Under their attack I began to feel hurt, defensive, and angry, hard as the latter was to admit. Perhaps I showed it in the discussion, although I tried not to. In the experience itself and in subsequent reflection upon it, I could not get away from the fact that, in spite of everything, these students perceived me as an American. Nor could I dismiss my own feeling that what they said about America was said also about me.

I thus had my first dramatic lesson in what it means to be part of a specific people. Other lessons followed. Some of them during my international life were similar to the discussion with the Indian students. Others happened after I returned to the United States in the sixties and, with many others, had to cope with the explosions in the American sense of identity which those years brought to the fore.

Other experiences took place in the course of achieving a far more extensive psychological self-knowledge than I had previously had. And the curious, withdrawn, and unimaginative decade of the seventies did not permit the question to lie fallow: What does it mean to be a part of a people?

On board ship from Joppa to Tarshish, Jonah was questioned by a captain and crew terrified by a storm. " 'Tell us, on whose account this evil has come upon us? What is your occupation? And whence do you come? What is your country? And of what people are you?' And he said to them, 'I am a Hebrew; and I fear the Lord, the God of heaven, who made the sea and the dry land' " (Jon. 1:8–9). Many of us today might have immediately first answered the crew's question about occupation. Not Jonah; his identity was established by reference to his people and his people's God. In Scripture personal identity is provided by the people and their faith.

Behind Jonah's reply lies Israel's monumental quest for its identity. This quest has its roots in the moments during many centuries when God's graciousness was made known. The way this happened varied. It happened through specific persons, through the ancient and continuing practice of worship, and through the growing traditions of the people. The quest began with the patriarchs, with Abraham, Isaac, and Jacob and the promise of blessing, posterity, and land. In clearer historical experience the quest took a giant leap forward when the Israelites were in Egypt:

> When the Lord saw that he turned aside to see, God called to him out of the bush, "Moses, Moses!" And he said, "Here am I." Then he said, "Do not come near; put off your shoes from your feet, for the place on which you are standing is holy ground." And he said, "I am the God of your father, the God of Abraham, the God of Isaac, and the God of Jacob." And Moses hid his face, for he was afraid to look at God. . . . Then the Lord said, ". . . now, behold, the cry of the people of Israel has come to me, and I have seen the oppression with which the Egyptians oppress them. Come, I will send you to Pharaoh that you may bring forth my people, the sons of Israel, out of Egypt." (Exod. 3:4–6; 7; 9–10)

From this occasion onward, identity took form as a people was fashioned. The circumstances varied and extended over a period of some twelve hundred and fifty years. The Exodus. Desert wanderers under Moses' genius. Settlement and development in Canaan among other peoples. David. Solomon in all his glory. The Temple. The great prophets, speaking to the people of past, present, and future. The influence of cultures and the gathering of wisdom. Division and misfortune. The impact of empires. Exile. Destruction. Return.

In this long, diverse experience, the Exodus had the force of a fundamental disclosure of Israel's identity. This afflicted people had been chosen to be delivered, to be faithful, and to be righteous in God's sight. So decisive was this event that it became a core tradition.[1] Other events, memories, and traditions were added to it. Sacred commandments gave concrete meaning to the originating experience, showing that obedience to this law gave this people its identity. The recounting of history from theological perspectives, as in the books of Samuel, Kings, and Chronicles, further explained the meaning of Israel's having been chosen by God. The prophets, for whom God's presence and speech were all but overpowering, did not depart from this core, but interpreted it. Israel's origins are clearly visible, for instance, in the words of the prophet of the exile who wrote late in the history, at a time of acute suffering. The people who had hitherto been certain of themselves seemed to have lost everything in captivity in Babylon. The prophet's words about the servant of the Lord[2] impart deepened meaning to the original calling:

"I am the Lord, I have called you in righteousness,
  I have taken you by the hand and kept you;
I have given you as a covenant to the people,
  a light to the nations . . ." (Isa. 42:6)

Thus the experience which constituted the people Israel did not fade, but rather lived, validated and reinvigorated by the impact of God's graciousness upon varied human experience. The initial event and the continuing process provided the basic knowledge: peoplehood is primary; human identity is found in the people and its peoplehood. The contrast between despair and praise expressed in Psalm 22 presents eloquent testimony to the meaning of the peoplehood and its origins:

My God, my God, why hast thou forsaken me?
Why art thou so far from helping me, from the words of my groaning?
O my God, I cry by day, but thou dost not answer;
  and by night, but find no rest.

I will tell of thy name to my brethren;
  in the midst of the congregation I will praise thee:
You who fear the Lord, praise him!
  all you sons of Jacob, glorify him,
  and stand in awe of him, all you sons of Israel!
For he has not despised or abhorred
  the affliction of the afflicted;
and he has not hid his face from him,
  but has heard, when he cried to him. (Ps. 22:1-2, 22-24)

As the Old Testament speaks of the ancient people, the New Testament speaks of a new people. This people, very small at first, was composed of individuals who had found a new identity because of Christ's impact upon them. From the first Easter moments, however, this happened within a sense of the group, which soon became a sense of people. The New Testament books, which began to be written about twenty years after Jesus' death, are not only products of the experience of their authors and editors but of the community itself—its traditions about Jesus remembered and passed along, its affirmations used in worship, and its accounts and interpretations of events in community life. Even Paul, the most dominant of the authors, is unthinkable apart from the new community.

The new people did not forget either Abraham or Moses, either the promise or the Exodus, but understood their meaning to be transformed. God was the same for them and their forefathers; but now, by means of Jesus Christ, God disclosed a new deliverance for all of humankind. The kingdom of God bespeaks a community, a people, ultimately all the peoples of humanity, in a transformed, consummated form. The concrete evidence of the kingdom of God for this early group was a new people. The persons who participated in it were aware of a new form of human existence, the life together in Christ, the supreme identity to which humans are called by God. One aspect of this was an acute interior struggle as the new identity in Christ was, in Paul's phrase, "put on"; yet this struggle resulted in an exultant power and freedom let loose by the new identity. Even so, the New Testament preserves the Old Testament structure. The fulfillment or transformation announced in the New Testament carries forward ancient Israel's knowledge that human identity is found in the matrix of a people.

Neither the people Israel nor the new people in Christ, however, lived in isolation; both found themselves among other peoples. The following two passages speak of this primary aspect of human relationships. It will be noted that neither passage views humanity as an undifferentiated mass nor as an atomistic conglomeration of individuals. Rather, they understand that the primary form in which humanity lives and in which human history runs its course is embraced in the word "people" or "peoples."

"For you are a people holy to the Lord your God; the Lord your God has chosen you to be a people for his own possession, out of all the peoples that are on the face of the earth." (Deut. 7:6)

After they finished speaking, James replied, "Brethren, listen to me. Symeon has related how God first visited the Gentiles [peoples], to take out of them a people for his name. And with this the words of the prophets agree. . . ." (Acts 15:13–14)

The word "people," which is also translated in the Bible into the words "nation," "nations," or "Gentiles," refers to an obvious, experience-based human group among whom there is a union of a binding quality. In Scripture the word applies to such groups irrespective of their particular characteristics. A people is united by living together, sometimes as a tribe or a national unit of common ancestry, and sometimes as a political unit defined by history or by constitution. It is a broad term.[3]

So defined, it points to a long-developing historical and cultural process. In the ancient East villages appeared between the seventh and fifth millennium B.C.; neolithic Jericho led the area in civilization some five thousand years before Abraham. By the fifth to the third millenniums civilization had spread throughout the region. The Mesopotamian Empire and Egypt appeared by the third millennium, and, at its close, Israel came into being.[4] Then other empires arose— Assyria, Babylon, Greece, and Rome—with consequent effect upon smaller peoples. From the earliest times the centuries were disturbed by movements, migrations, and invasions which upset established patterns. Growth and change among peoples were endemic to the historical environment of the area and the time.

From within this ancient cradle of peoples and civilization, one people encountered the reality of God. The skeptic may say that they simply read into their religious experience a historical development, long in the making, to which they were unconsciously subject. Perhaps so, but that explanation would have to take into account a startling factor. This people believed that God heard their cry, met their affliction, and made them a people. "Then the Lord said, 'I have seen the affliction of my people who are in Egypt, and have heard their cry because of their taskmasters'" (Exod. 3:7). Walter Harrelson notes, "God's coming to the aid of a *people* under oppression has no counterpart in the ancient world."[5] The point is not merely their rescue from slavery, momentous as that is. The point is that in this experience with God a sense of identity was provided to a people, never to be forgotten. Through self-discovery Israel came to know something essential about humanity: the "people" in the matrix of human identity in general.

One is not usually exhilarated by reading Genesis 10, the Table of Nations, as it is called. It is a dry, improbable catalog. If, however, one backs off from its detail, this chapter offers a rewarding perspective. It belongs, in the happy phrase of Gerhard von Rad, to "primeval history."[6]

What can primeval history mean? Our home in central Minnesota is located on a long finger of hilly, rocky land which was pushed out by the glacial movements of the Ice Age. It is wooded land, and our house is in a forest. This land has remained unoccupied until now; rocks, clay, and forest are not conducive to farming. So far as local memory goes, the forest has been "logged over" twice in its history, the last time some twenty to thirty years ago. The forest is dense and tangled, but when the small growth is cleared out the great oaks, birches, and elms stand in visible splendor. On a still day in the summer, when the sun and heat are high, and also in the quiet evening of such a day, one can hear a hum in the forest—low pitched but insistent, the noise of millions of flying insects, mostly mosquitoes. I don't know when mosquitoes emerged into the world's environment, but modern insects were here in the Cretaceous Period, sixty-five to one hundred thirty-five million years ago. Within the insect hum the scurrying of the little animals sounds loud in the stillness, and deer watch through the foliage—mammals, present since the Paleocene Period. I stand there, silent of tongue and quieted in spirit, young in this scheme of things, yet knowing that my forebears walked on earth long before remembered history was known. This land, these trees, these insects, these animals stir the imagination. "This," wrote Longfellow, "is the forest primeval." From one's depths comes a sense of history that is not history.

In this fashion the stark, staccato words of the Table of Nations speak of the immemorial. In those words, peoples, cultures, achievements, and origins are described. The table makes clear that humanity is composed of peoples, and, as if to emphasize the point, Israel itself is not mentioned. It also indicates that crucial ingredients of what we call human identity are found in the matrix of peoples. Its power consists in being located in primeval history, in that time before remembered history of which imagination makes us aware. The imagination of those who recorded the meaning of Israel's tradition was set loose and informed by experience with God, an experience which enabled them to perceive the primordial essence of things human.

That essence is a people, a union of binding quality, a union which establishes the arena of creativity, provides continuity, and makes ordering possible. By implying these functions of people and peoplehood and by locating them in primeval history, Scripture suggests that people is a provision of God for human life. No doctrine of providence appears in the Table of Nations but rather the conviction that from this primeval time a fundamental structure for human life has been provided. From the reality of experience with God, Israel understood the reality of human life.

It is likely that the Table of Nations was finally formulated during the time of the great prophets. The prophets provide drama and power to the insight embodied in the table. Amos's passion runs high. In a fury derived from love of God's justice, he turns to various peoples, to Damascus, Gaza, Tyre, the Ammonites, Moab, and then to Judah and Israel, denouncing them for the cruelties which they perpetuate within themselves or inflict upon others or both. With these people and also with others, Isaiah, Jeremiah, and Ezekiel do the same.[7] They too speak of specific evils—of devastating injustice, of cruelties and imperialism—but they do not speak, as moderns do, of "issues." They speak to peoples about peoples and their identity. What the Table of Nations registers as being provided by God the prophets address in the name of God.

The New Testament carries forward this view of people and peoples. Indeed, that is one reason why the New Testament can scarcely be understood apart from the Old. The New Testament speaks briefly, with allusions which presuppose the Old Testament knowledge. The result is a different view of the people of God and its relation to the peoples of the world, but not a new view of humanity. "People in general do not exist," writes Paul Minear about the New Testament. "There are only particular peoples. Each people has a separate and cohesive actuality of its own. Every person belongs to a particular people, just as he belongs to a particular tongue or nation or tribe; and this people is not reducible to the mathematical aggregate of its members. The people defines the person; its existence is determinative of who he is. Hence, when an individual shifts from one people to another, a drastic change in his status and selfhood is involved."[8]

This background gives bite to Acts 15:13–14, cited earlier, which says that the new people of God is drawn from the peoples of the earth. That involves a shift from one identity to a new identity in the people of Christ. Thus the gospel is to be preached to peoples, and human history is consummated as peoples enter the kingdom of God (Matt. 25:31–46). Our familiarity with such phrases should not beguile us into thinking that this use of "people" and of "peoples" is casual, resulting from natural convenience, a conventional world view, or a manner of speaking. This usage rises from the deep structure of the tradition that perceived that God creates not only the covenant people but peoples and peoplehood everywhere.

Scripture speaks of God and God's ways; yet because Scripture speaks of God, it speaks of a people and of peoples. God hears, addresses, constitutes, and leads a people, whether that be the people led by Moses or the people in Christ. God's graciousness produces a people. The irreducible element in the whole is the knowledge that human beings achieve identity within peoples and have a primary relationship to God as peoples. Speaking of God's presence, Samuel Terrien writes: "Presence is that which creates a people. Presence is the reality to which man must attune himself if he is to live at all, for there is not solitary life. The family and tribe grow into a welded society. The Hebraic notion of 'peoplehood' represents a new reality in the history of mankind. . . . Presence is the root of 'peoplehood.'"[9]

5

Peoples: Creativity and Character

Two further words are associated with Scripture's treatment of peoples: "creativity" and "character." Like "identity," both are dependent upon the primal element of peoplehood and are decisive components of it.

Peoplehood is the matrix of creativity. The Table of Nations, we noted, refers to the cultural achievements of peoples. That means creativity. This recognition of diverse human creativity and achievement in primeval history puts one in mind of Margaret Mead's discussion of the distinguishing mark of Homo sapiens: "It is customary to say that man is a culture-building animal. . . . It might be more useful to say that Homo sapiens is a species which can only survive in a man-made environment, using man's dependence on a culture as the species-characteristic statement. . . . Man may then be said to be a culture-living creature."[1] That conclusion is akin to the scriptural view. Survival only in a "man-made environment" suggests that some form of living together, some form of people, is a necessity of human life. "Dependence on a culture" indicates the inherent capacity and need to create and to rely upon the results of creativity. A "culture-living creature" implies that the people, created from living together and the bond that results, is the matrix in which human creativity takes place.

Although one notes that culture and creativity as such are not mentioned in Scripture, peoples and their cultures are. Scripture takes creativity and culture seriously. A culture rose in contrast to other cultures because a people had been chosen and sent on its way. The laws, legends, and history of the Torah contain much that one may call cultural; yet Torah was for Israel the revealed will of God. No separation appeared between God's will and cultural creativity as such. On the contrary, the Ten Commandments include cultural imperatives: "Honor your father and your mother. . . . You shall not covet" (Exod. 20:12, 17). David and Solomon were expressions, personally and symbolically, of Israel's creativity. The wisdom literature moves in a broad cultural spectrum, yet it is set within the frame of the ancient people. Even foreign cultures, for instance Babylon under Cyrus, are understood to be the instrument of God. And, in the New Testament, the cultures of Israel, the Greeks, and the Romans come into play both directly and indirectly. Human creativity and its cultural result do figure heavily in Scripture.

The reason is not hard to find. Scripture treats cultural achievement theologically, in the same way that it treats history. What people create in their life together affects the bond that unites them; in the long run a people's creativity displays its identity. The chosen people may not worship golden calves, but they may use music in their worship of God. The difference is that the worship of cultural creativity is idolatry, but music used in worship serves God. Cultural creativity is part of peoplehood but not a part of it to which God is indifferent. Moreover, the creativity of a people implies and leads to its character.

We are thus brought to a further term. Peoplehood is the matrix of identity; as such, peoplehood is the matrix of creativity; and, we suggest, it is also the matrix of character. Although the word "character" is not prominent in Scripture, the reality of the word is.

Israel's identity not only implied but demanded a certain character. Read from this viewpoint, the Old Testament is a continuing dialogue concerning God and the people's character. Although the latter was in fact sometimes winsome and sometimes not so attractive, the purpose of the Torah was to produce joyful and faithful living with God.[2] No leader—Moses, judge, or king—stood in between the people and God. People were expected to respond to God with their life and loyalty in specific relationships within the community. This expectation broadly defined a certain character. In one mode, character was also outlined by the demands of sacred commandments; in another, by the praise, confession, and petition of worship. In yet a further mode, character was indicated by the Word, spoken directly to some who then passed it on. And, in all modes of the divine dialogue with Israel about character, renewed experience of God's graciousness revitalized memory of its origins.

Similarly, as Christ inaugurated the new era of the kingdom of God, creating a new people to be a sign of its coming, and as henceforth this people identified itself by reference to Christ and the kingdom he installed, this identity demanded a certain character. The New Testament from this viewpoint is panoramic, presenting different views of the same landscape. Varied descriptions of the character of the new people come forth: the people of God, the new creation, the body of Christ, and many others.[3] One must remember that the New Testament books were written out of the actual experience of being a new people in Christ. A new people had come to be, and virtually every word of the people's writings is a clue to its character—its faith, practice, thought, common life, mission, hope. The accent everywhere is upon character, but not character as something in and of itself. Character is the touchstone of the new being, the evidence that the life in Christ is a different life, a distinctive mode of existence, a new identity fashioned within a new people.

Character is thus never abstracted from peoplehood. On the contrary, peoplehood sets the stage for a fundamental coherence in the human drama. In it identity, creativity, and character imply and affect one another. None can exist alone. Peoplehood and identity are empty without creativity and character; creativity and character are formless without peoplehood and identity. Yet character is the clue to all. It is Scripture's bottom line; it registers the coherence of the whole.

Peoplehood requires two distinctive marks of character. Without them, Scripture says severely, the whole structure falls; peoplehood dries up into "no people."[4] The first important characteristic is faithfulness to God: "Hear, O Israel: The Lord our God is one Lord; and you shall love the Lord your God with all your heart, and with all your soul, and with all your might" (Deut. 6:4–5). Here, in the Shema, one senses more than correct doctrine. The loyalty it commands exhibits an edge of fierceness which shrivels all other loyalties. Nowhere is this more vividly portrayed than in the account of Elijah's encounter with the Canaanite prophets of Baal (1 Kings 18:17–40), which registers the transcendent conviction that any god other than Yahweh is likely to be sleeping at the moment of need and should have little or no serious claim upon a people's loyalty. In Jesus' view the priority that put the kingdom of God first in a person's faithfulness removed anxiety concerning even food, drink, and clothing (Matt. 6:25–34). The substance of biblical monotheism lies in the conviction that only God is God, whether the challenge comes from the gods of human culture or the gods of inner anxieties. Because Scripture understands that peoplehood derives from God, it insists that peoplehood respect, adhere to, and participate in that monotheism. Other gods, external or internal, destroy the peoplehood. The quality of peoplehood and the character engendered by it are not ordinary. The mystery of God causes other loyalties to fade before the supreme loyalty; the clarity of God's graciousness endows the peoplehood with a character not achievable by the people itself, namely, an extraordinary faithfulness.

The second trait of character is presented in a clear scriptural theme. A true people must care and provide for the afflicted and the oppressed. This character of peoplehood is built into the origin of the ancient people itself. God heard the cry of the afflicted and delivered the oppressed from their suffering. Stated differently, the cry of the oppressed is the cry that God hears; that cry is the concern of God; the answer to that cry discloses the nature of God's love. This character of the peoplehood is in the law,[5] and if to latter-day ears specific laws seem oppressive, it must be kept in mind that nevertheless the memory of Egypt was constant. It is found in the prophets, who turn the divine Word upon the injustice of Israel and Judah in favor of the oppressed, proclaiming release for the captives. This concern of God is also in the gospel. There, in both symbolic and literal ways, the demand for the character of the people reaches supreme expression. Symbolically, it stands at the beginning and at the end of the good news. Literally, the demand is explicit.

Luke inaugurates Jesus' birth with the praise by Mary:

"My soul magnifies the Lord,
and my spirit rejoices in God my Savior,
for he has regarded the low estate of his handmaiden.
For behold, henceforth all generations will call me blessed;
for he who is mighty has done great things for me,

and holy is his name.
And his mercy is on those who fear him
from generation to generation.
He has shown strength with his arm,
he has scattered the proud in the imagination of their hearts,
he has put down the mighty from their thrones,
and exalted those of low degree;
he has filled the hungry with good things,
and the rich he has sent empty away.
He has helped his servant Israel,
in remembrance of his mercy,
as he spoke to our fathers,
to Abraham and his posterity for ever." (Luke 1:46–55)

The Gospel of Matthew concludes Jesus' discourse on the kingdom of God with his account of the last judgment:

"Before him will be gathered all the nations, and he will separate them one from another as the shepherd separates the sheep from the goats, and he will place the sheep at his right hand, but the goats at the left. Then the King will say to those at his right hand, 'Come, O blessed of my Father, inherit the kingdom prepared for you from the foundation of the world; for I was hungry and you gave me food, I was thirsty and you gave me drink, I was a stranger and you welcomed me, I was naked and you clothed me, I was sick and you visited me, I was in prison and you came to me.' Then the righteous will answer him, 'Lord, when did we see thee hungry and feed thee, or thirsty and give thee drink? And when did we see thee a stranger and welcome thee, or naked and clothe thee?' And the King will answer them, 'Truly, I say to you, as you did it to one of the least of these my brethren, you did it to me.'" (Matt. 25:32–40)

No one comment, no one thesis can exhaust the meaning or resonance of these passages. They stand as statements of character: the people of God, if it is true to its calling, is this kind of people. So forcefully does this appear in Scripture that it comes to be a crucial standard of the character of a people.

Is this whimsical? The idiosyncrasy of a people who was oppressed and wanted out? A tradition which, however magnificently expressed and transformed, lacks coherence with the whole? Is love of the dispossessed a mere option, to be taken up, perhaps, by a few "saints" who have a special mandate? Or does care of the oppressed have a place within the whole?

Two words are critical in the reply to these questions. The first is
"experience"; the second is "coherence." Experience refers to Israel's
knowledge that God heard . . . and saw . . . and led. This experience
goes far beyond the natural human desire to "get out," for it led into
such unexpected realms, invited such transformed understanding,
and inaugurated such renewed vitality of life that the participants in
this experience understood it to have originated from the Holy One,
from God, from reality itself. On the basis of this experience, love of the
dispossessed is not optional. Experience refers to the impact of Jesus
upon his followers: he came to them in the "form of a servant."[6] He was
"Christ the Lord," and, indeed, known in many other ways and by
other terms; yet throughout all there runs the persistent theme of
Jesus the servant, obedient unto death. To whom, however, was this
man a servant? In preaching, healing, teaching he addressed all; his
death was for all. The "all" included everyone, expecially those who
might well have been overlooked or excluded. On the basis of the
experience of Jesus as servant, love of the dispossessed is not merely
optional.

With experience, which refers to experience of God and Christ,
goes coherence. Release for the captivies has coherence with God's
providing peoplehood. With startling clarity, care for the dispossessed—demonstrated from the cry in Egypt to the life in Christ—
simultaneously shows us the essence of peoplehood and provides the
test case by which to measure the character of peoplehood. To dispossess, subjugate, oppress, or deprive a person or group by neglect is to
deny peoplehood to that person or group. To do this is to push them to
the margins of the bond that unites, margins at which the air is too thin
for breathing. It is to make of them "no people" or at best people on the
edge of life and survival. As noted by Thomas Hoyt, who as a Black
knows what life on the margin of American society is like, it is a
mistake to believe that God is "on the side of the poor" because they
have a special virtue.[7] The issue runs deeper. Scripture bears mighty
testimony to the fact that to dispossess people, to disown or treat them
as if they did not "belong," is to cut them off from the peoplehood by
which their identity as humans is made possible. The irony is that
dispossession is never complete; the oppressed remain captives,
whose ceiling is somebody else's floor. That is why God is on their side.

They suffer because their human identity is cruelly truncated; they do not have access to the very thing that provides true humanity. Thus response to God's love for the dispossessed is neither whimsy nor idiosyncrasy. It is the crucial measure of the capacity of any peoplehood to nurture a truly human people.

It must not be thought that Scripture's attention to the character of a people, and all that is implied by that, is confined to the convenant people. Israel and the church are the focus, but the focus does not foreshorten the range of vision. From the experience in Egypt onward, other peoples are in view. The attention given to them, from Pharaoh in the Old Testament to "all peoples" in the New, makes clear that Yahweh is the God of all. The meaning of that for the identity and character of peoples as a whole is less clear than it is for the covenant peoples, save for one strong impression, namely, that any people can, and do, go too far in the perversion of peoplehood. Therein is the force of the prophets' address to Israel's neighbors and of the parable of the last judgment in Matthew 25. Both focus upon peoples whose character has gone too far awry. And one feels something more. Is there not the further implication here that among peoples of such character something has gone radically wrong at the center, at the point where their faith and loyalty, however it may be expressed, has strayed too greatly from the reality of all life? In any case, "going too far" has a specific meaning: being too unjust, too cruel, too rapacious, and too neglectful of the dispossessed. It means doing those things that violate character, distort culture, and fragment human identity to so marked a degree that those who do them are not worthy to be called a people. Moreover, whether that happens among the covenant people or elsewhere, God cares. From the primeval history to Jesus' inauguration of the kingdom of God, Scripture is clear that God's graciousness embraces the conditon of peoples everywhere. Character is united to creativity, identity, and peoplehood not only for Israel and the church but for all peoples as well.

6

People and Person

How is the person related to the people and the people to the person? In general, people and peoplehood provide the matrix for human identity, creativity, and character. Even so, does the person have a real place, or is the person a cog in the collective machine?

The basic answer comes indirectly, from Scripture's knowledge of God rather than from a calculation of the balance between the person and the collective people. The underlying stratum, the essence of Scripture's disclosure, is God's love for human beings. That love strongly reaches the person through the people;[1] but however strongly Scripture speaks of the people and of peoples, God's love comes to persons.

The prophet Jeremiah uttered landmark words as to the manner in which God's purpose and love reached persons. Like others in the prophetic tradition, he spoke to peoples and of peoples. Yet he spoke of something new, a new perception of the bondage by which a human being is held in self-opposition to God. This in turn led Jeremiah to decry a new form of the relation of God to humanity.

> "Behold, the days are coming, says the Lord, when I will make a new covenant with the house of Israel and the house of Judah. . . . But this is the covenant which I will make with the house of Israel after those days, says the Lord: I will put my law within them, and I will write it upon their hearts; and I will be their God, and they shall be my people." (Jer. 31:31, 33)

Jeremiah knew well what had happened to the peoplehood, identity, creativity, and character of Israel:

44

"Why then has this people turned away
  in perpetual backsliding?
They hold fast to deceit,
  they refuse to return.
I have given heed and listened,
  but they have not spoken aright;
no man repents of his wickedness,
  saying, 'What have I done?'
Every one turns to his own course,
  like a horse plunging headlong into battle." (Jer. 8:5–6)

Jeremiah also knew the utter love of God:

"Thus says the Lord, the God of Israel: Like these good figs, so I will
regard as good the exiles from Judah, whom I have sent away from this
place to the land of the Chaldeans. I will set my eyes upon them for good,
and I will bring them back to this land. I will build them up, and not tear
them down; I will plant them, and not uproot them. I will give them a
heart to know that I am the Lord; and they shall be my people and I will be
their God, for they shall return to me with their whole heart." (Jer. 24:4–7)

Jeremiah has been interpreted as setting forth a new individualism,
and in one sense he did. His individualism, however, does not abstract
the individual from the structure of God and the people; rather, it gives
the person a true relationship to the people. Deceitful, refusing to
return, not repenting of wickedness, turning to their own course like a
horse plunging headlong into battle—such had the people Israel become. These conditions betrayed a perversion of the peoplehood from
within the heart and bespoke people trapped in their own self-rebellion
against God and the people of God. Only God's law on the inward
perversion of this peoplehood, on the heart corrupted by the falling
away, would suffice.[2] To Jeremiah, God's love meant that they would
be given a heart free from this bondage, a heart to be God's people.
God's love, law, and purpose within a person do not dispense with
God's creation of a people; instead they mean a new peoplehood rooted
in the heart. This new covenant makes clear that there is a reciprocal
relationship between the person and the people. A social bond remains; God creates a people whose bond is loyalty to God. Yet that
social bond is not external. Peoplehood exists within and cannot be
abstracted from the person.

The structure of Jeremiah's insight is expanded and transformed in

the New Testament. Jeremiah spoke of God's law—God's will for
Israel—being written on the heart; the New Testament speaks of
God's will for a new people to which the heart is called to respond. The
New Testament is concerned with a distinct people: the people of the
kingdom of God, present now and coming in the future, a consummated humanity. Thus the final scriptural word gathers up the
primordial fact: even in consummated form, humanity requires community. The shift in the character and future of human existence
accomplished by Christ is a shift in peoplehood.

That shift is accomplished as persons enter the peoplehood of God's
kingdom. The conditions for entrance are stated by Jesus in three
words addressed directly to each individual: repent, believe, and follow.

> Now after John was arrested, Jesus came into Galilee, preaching the
> gospel of God, and saying, "The time is fulfilled, and the kingdom of God is
> at hand; repent, and believe in the gospel." (Mark 1:14)

> And he called to him the multitude with his disciples, and said to them, "If
> any man would come after me, let him deny himself and take up his cross
> and follow me." (Mark 8:34)

Therein lie the conditions of the heart required for entrance into the
new people. These conditions summarize the person's relation to God.
Repent—turn to God. Believe—accept and trust in God. Follow—
commit oneself to God who is in Christ. The center for it all is the
trusting heart. I cannot repent unless I trust the One to whom I turn. I
cannot follow unless I trust the One who is in Christ and the Christ
who is in the One.

This highly personal relation to God, however, turns around one
question: What peoplehood exists in the heart? The conditions for
entrance into the kingdom of God are more than admittance creden-
tials. Something happens to the repentant, believing, and following
heart. The person enters the new community because a new form of
peoplehood begins to emerge in the innermost parts. In the New
Testament understanding, however, this community is not founded
and does not grow as individuals join, plan, and promote it in the way
social organizations are created. Individuals may join one by one, and
sometimes by groups, but always—even from the earliest times—with

the consciousness of entering something already there. This community is given, not only in the sense of its already being there but also and supremely in the sense of its being a gift. It has been given in both senses since the surprised disciples met Christ after his death and others met the Spirit of God-in-Christ at Pentecost (Acts 2:1ff.). In this community persons find their identity in Christ, are empowered to engage in the new creativity, and discover that the character of Christ in some measure becomes their own character. The peoplehood of God's kingdom is written within. A new form of human survival, a new culture-dependence, a new culture-living process, takes the place of the old.

My engagement in 1957 with the Indian students could be interpreted in purely political terms. I believe, however, that the encounter registered deeper than that. Indian independence from British rule had been achieved only ten years earlier; the great traditions and dignity of the Indian people were joined with high aspirations for the future. After a long, stagnant, subjugated period, a renewed sense of peoplehood was alive. Experiencing this renewal when talking to the Indian students, I found my own peoplehood aroused, for I too come from an independent people proud of its achievements. However, I was also conscious of my origins because during the conversation there was a sense of threat and of being threatened, of attack and of being attacked. The reason for these feelings was not simply that the students felt that U.S. policy threatened India. Rather, it seemed that the United States, and I as an American, threatened them in a deeper way. Similarly, what the students said about the United States did not come across impersonally; it seemed to be said about me, and my responses seemed to be taken personally by them. In that small meeting the issue was not policy but the claims of peoplehood. In a way that probably no one understood, the meeting poignantly exposed one of the basic conditions for human life.

As Scripture records the wondrous modes in which God's graciousness comes to human beings, it speaks of people and peoples with such consistency and emphasis as to warrant a fundamental conclusion: these terms designate a constant element in human existence. This constant condition of human life was not discovered by observation (although it may be confirmed both by common sense and by science) but by the recognition of the effect of God's graciousness upon human beings. From experience and knowledge of the ultimate God comes experience and knowledge of the essence of human life. In order to exist at all, humans must exist as peoples. People and peoples are thus a constant of human life and existence, known because God is first known. What does this mean? Three answers form the response.

First, people and peoples signify a constant condition of human existence. A people is any group formed by persons living together and given cohesion by a common bond. Humanity is composed of peoples. The groups may be as large as the Roman Empire or as small as Samaria. Scripture allows for an almost infinite variety of peoples, and there is no evidence that Scripture desires to see any one form of peoplehood dominate the earth. The vision of the kingdom of God embraces the peoples in a consummated relationship with God; it does not call for some form of universal civilization. On the other hand, humanity is not conceived of as only a mass of individuals. The individual figures in supreme measure, but the individual as such is not the category by which Scripture treats humanity. Instead, the individual finds true life within the basic human reality suggested by the terms "people" and "peoples."

Second, people and peoples are not only the primary form in which humanity exists, but they are also the matrix in which indispensable needs of human life are met. In this sense also peoples are a constant in the human condition. One cannot be human without achieving a form of personal identity, and that is accomplished by virtue of the people. One cannot be human without engaging in the creativity that provides for life; that is also accomplished by virtue of the people. Scripture sees clearly that these functions arise from the processes of living together and from the common bond uniting those so engaged. Scripture does not accent the social side of life. Scripture tells us with all the power at its disposal that there is no human life save life together; the identity, creativity, and character that make humans "human" result from life shared in a common bond. Similarly, Scripture states plainly that as these positive aspects of life arise from the people, so the people is the matrix in which the deterioration of these human fundamentals takes place. Thus, where there is a deterioration in character, a slackening in creativity, and uncertainty in identity, Scripture directs one to examine the peoplehood, the bond that unites, and the processes of living within that bond. When human problems appear, the essential difficulty or corruption lies in that bond.

Third, people and peoples are a constant of human existence because peoplehood is the means of renewal of both person and people. If deterioration results from dry rot at the center, from a corruption in the common bond that joins people, then renewal comes with the forging of a new bond. Human beings must become a true people. That is the appeal Scripture makes. It does not mean adjusting this, that, or another aspect of the psyche, personality, or one's social life. When Scripture speaks of a renewal of peoplehood, it means a revision or recasting of the bond that unites. When the bond comes round right, other adjustments become right. Scripture never tires of its fundamental point· renewal among humans has to do with achieving the right bond to unite them in their life as peoples.

7

The Beginning of Spirituality:
Peoplehood as a Boundary
of the Human Spirit

In the spring of my first year at Yale Divinity School, I sat in the course on the history of Christian doctrine. The professor was Robert L. Calhoun, revered by generations of Yale students. One morning brought the conclusion of a presentation on John Calvin. Following his usual method, Professor Calhoun had carefully summarized Calvin's thought, locating it in the currents of the time and tracing its connections to preceding history. Evaluation followed. After appropriate tribute to Calvin, Professor Calhoun then turned to criticism. The criticism—so far as my now distant memory goes—focused vigorously on predestination, for which the professor had little love. Then came an arresting sentence. It was to the effect that however one evaluates the belief that God predestines us each to salvation or damnation we cannot escape altogether a general idea of being predestined. This idea has one firm base in observable human experience, namely, that we cannot escape the time and place in which we were born.

In chapters 4, 5, and 6 we discovered that we cannot escape being part of a peoplehood at a specific time of its development. We were born into it. This fact lies behind the purpose of chapters 7, 8, and 9. In them we explore the implications of people and peoples for Christian spirituality, starting our discussion with the beginning of spirituality: peoplehood as a boundary of the spirit.

We noted in chapter 3 that God's graciousness becomes known in the midst of life, and that one result is a certain self-awareness and knowledge. Further, Scripture makes it plain that this self-knowledge has an effect. It strips away all illusions of grandeur, whether subtle or gross, and puts in their place a firm comprehension that life is limited and that each person operates within its inexorable limitations. One of these limits, suggested by Professor Calhoun's remark, is that we are each born into a specific people.

Before proceeding it should be pointed out that peoplehood exists at different levels. The base line, however, is clear: a people is marked off or defined by whatever common bond unites it. This bond is distinctive and serves to identify the people, whichever one it may be. But this distinctive identification by a common bond does not mean that a people is compartmentalized or immune from the influence of other peoples. Various levels of influence suggest that the bond that unites any one people may consist of intermingled dimensions.

Scripture is not precise at this point, for it does not have a high level of direct sociological interest. It speaks symbolically, as in the Table of Nations, and politically, as when it refers, for instance, to Pharaoh and Egypt, Sennacherib and Assyria, Cyrus and Babylon, Caesar and Rome. It refers to cultures and to struggles between them, as when Israel entered Canaan to find its life there. The prophets, concerned with the spiritual conditions and moral practices of all kinds of peoples, make it clear that from the greatest empires to the smallest tribes God is the Lord of all. And Scripture allows that distinct peoples may exist within other peoples, as the Israelites existed within Rome. Overall, the vocation of the people of God, whether ancient Israel or the church, is to be true to its own peoplehood within the varied peoples of the world.

In Scripture we also encounter different levels of peoplehood. Scriptural development took place in the eastern Mediterranean world in which, as we earlier noted, the influence of varied peoples upon one another had for millenniums been the warp and woof of human experience. Our life is similar, except that because of communications our consciousness is becoming increasingly global. Western, Islamic, Marxist, Hindu, and Buddhist civilizations all present distinct peoples on a large scale; and if one thinks geographically of Asia, Africa, Europe, North America, and Latin America, other perspectives come into play. If in this panorama one descries great peoples or civilizations distinguished by common bonds, one is also aware that smaller peoples exist within the larger. Western civilization, for instance, includes the European peoples organized into nation-states and their counterparts in North America, Australia, and New Zealand. Within them there are also distinct peoples—Slovaks, Alsatians, and the Welsh, for instance, and the many ethnic groups in the United States. The effect is a layered peoplehood which, like layered clothing (perhaps itself a symbol?), adds up to an ensemble.[1] Most remain within the people of their birth. Yet millions move from one people to another, whether in this century of the homeless person[2] for reasons of violence or in this era of migration by reason of choice. Although it has always been true, it is dramatically true in the modern world that intercultural penetration adds layer to layer so that the ensemble shifts even within a lifetime, producing the promise of enrichment while simultaneously resulting in change and disturbance.

Scripture does not lament but rather accepts the existence of many specific peoples. This acceptance is eloquent in itself, and it has two consequences. First, unlike Plato's *Republic* and other idealisms and unlike all imperialisms of the past and present that claim that their form of peoplehood is "the best," Scripture does not insist that all peoples adopt a uniform civilization. Variety among peoples is an asset; it is the expression of creativity. Second, acceptance of a variety of peoples produces hope and realism. In the contemporary world many protest that tribalism, nationalism, and imperialism are the bane of our time, posing in their place the desirability of a world civilization to inhabit the global village. Scripture is seriously against large or small imperialisms, but it recognizes the place of peoples and peoplehood in human history and extends the hope of a transformation which will enable them to live together in peace.

Peoplehood, we suggested in chapter 6, is a constant element in human life. However layered it may be, a people is: (1) necessary to existence; (2) the matrix in which identity, creativity, and character are fashioned and expressed; and (3) a focal point of renewal in the basic functions of life. Taken together, these three characteristics spell out the meaning of "constant." We humans cannot get away from these aspects of peoplehood.

At the same time, peoples and peoplehood are a limit to life, not only in ways that are theoretical and abstract but in ways that are specific and concrete. It is easy to forget that this is so. From one viewpoint, the peoples of humanity are a glory: the panorama of humanity's peoples and civilizations displays an energy, inventiveness, and variety which lifts the imagination. No wonder that one may discern the image of God in human beings, no wonder that the human is but "a little lower than the angels"! When we participate in a people, find its sense of identity, and feel its stir of creative powers, the sense of limit is remote.

From another perspective, however, the human need to live as peoples is an inescapable limit to human capacities. First, each person is, and must be, born into a specific people, into one of the varieties of common bond that unites human beings. That sets the stage for the individual. It is a big stage, and it accommodates a seemingly infinite variety of individual dramas. Yet these personal dramas unfold on the same stage and so have properties in common. In America, for instance, we do not act out our personal dramas on either a medieval European or modern Japanese stage. We have our own style, as do others everywhere. Even in a process of changing one's people, whether as an immigrant or as a refugee, one moves from this people to that one without escaping the influence of either.

The second limit inherent in peoplehood flows from the first. If no one can exist or develop human capacities save as a part of a people, this always means that one is defined by a particular peoplehood and no other. For me it means the layered American peoplehood. Only the American people at this time makes my existence possible; only it is the matrix for my identity, my creativity, my character, and my renewal. This limitation does not yield a doctrine of predestination, but it does carry the overtones of it, of being captive not only to peoplehood in general but to the form of it into which one is born.

One might derive fatalism from that fact. Scripture does say "and that's the way it is," not only on one evening but throughout human history. With that in mind one might think that Scripture supports the view that each of us, and humanity as a whole, is subject to a blind, collective fate—that the panorama of peoples is determined by historical forces beyond anyone's control and that individuals are fated by the destiny of their particular peoplehood. That, however, is not so.

We might be closer to the spirit of Scripture if instead of limit we spoke of boundary. When reading of God's great visitations to Moses, Isaiah, and others, seeing in the visitations both God's mystery as well as God's clarity, one is impressed with a sense of boundary, a point beyond human capacities, a line at which the person is met. During the 1947–48 Indonesian war for independence, two men, colleagues in the ecumenical movement and friends of mine,[3] visited that country to express their concern for peace and freedom. They began their visit in the area held by the Dutch. Desiring to greet the fighters for independence, they were then taken to the front line. There the Dutch escorts had to stop; they could go no further. Venturing alone into a strip of no man's land, my friends were met by representatives of the other side. A boundary of warfare had been crossed so that two emissaries of peace could be met. In similar fashion, Scripture testifies that at the boundaries of human life we are met not by the hostilities of warfare but by the graciousness of God.

Peoplehood is one boundary of human life, but it is also one constant point at which God redeems life. Scripture is a record of those who have broken through the limits of peoplehood. The authors of Scripture knew that there is something beyond peoples. They knew that God creates peoples, God wants renewed peoples, and that, in the consummation of human history, God wants all peoples made new.

God's desires contain two promises. When God is sought inwardly, where our peoplehood is inscribed, there God meets the person. When God is sought at the outer boundaries of our peoplehood, as when the people cried to God in Egypt, there God meets the people. Then the great vista opens. God is known—Lord of history, of history in the person and of person in the history. Hope for release arises for the captives. The constant limit of human peoplehood is not absolute or final; it is an enduring point at which God's graciousness operates.

8

The Content
of Spirituality:
Identity in Christ

What does God's graciousness at the boundary of peoplehood entail for Christian spirituality?

From among the peoples, God has brought forth a new people in Christ. One intent of New Testament Christians was that the people of Christ exist among the many peoples of the world. The clear mandate that the gospel be preached to and lived among the world's peoples gives the framework for one fundamental aspect of Christian spirituality: movement from orientation in one's people of birth to orientation in the people of God.

We noted in chapter 4 that response to the gospel of Christ produces a shift in identity. One naturally expects those who follow Christ to have a certain type of character: for instance, one fashioned by love rather than by aggressive ambition or self-centered desire. One also recognizes that Christ's followers have a new context within which to express their personal creativity. They will participate in the kingdom of God rather than pursue fame or personal satisfaction. Underlying these characteristics, among others, is the action of entering and participating in the people of Christ, a distinctive peoplehood formed by the common bonding accomplished by God-in-Christ. Henceforth, that peoplehood provides the final or supreme matrix of the believer's life. One moves from a previous identity to an identity "in Christ."

What does an identity in Christ signify? I find illumination in the definition of identity offered by Erik Erikson, to whom I turn because of personal experience. In the late sixties my own life, or at least part of it, seemed to come apart, driven by inner forces which I did not understand and could not control. The situation reached the point of desperation, and being referred by others, I became a patient of Dr. Herbert Peyser in New York. After nearly a year of therapy, he asked one summer day whether I had ever read Erikson. I replied that I had never heard of him. "He made 'identity' a household word," Dr. Peyser replied. "Here, take this and read it." He gave me an early article by Erikson in which he sketched the concept of identity, and I read it with consuming excitement. I then turned to Erikson's 1968 book, *Identity: Youth and Crisis*. The book's concept of identity came to me as a kind of revelation. It made many other things intelligible and was a turning point for me in self-understanding.

Erikson's definition of identity illumines Christian spirituality at five points. Four of those points may be thought of as foundation stones that are indispensable to life in Christ. These points, however, are completed by a fifth point which concerns the importance and role of peoplehood, the interplay between the psychological and the social not only in human identity in general but in Christian spirituality in particular. For Erikson, identity consists of: (1) a subjective sense; (2) an invigorating continuity; (3) true self-discovery; (4) the failure of all guaranties; and (5) a lifelong process located at the core of the individual and the core of the person's communal nature. These points are contained in three quotations from Erikson's work.[1] We shall turn to those points and, in addition, to references from Scripture in order to suggest their connection to basic elements in Christian spirituality.

Erikson begins his definition of identity as follows:

> As a *subjective sense* of an *invigorating sameness* and *continuity*, what I would call a sense of identity seems to me best described by William James in a letter to his wife: "A man's character is discernible in the mental or moral attitude in which, when it came upon him, he felt himself most deeply and intensely alive. At such moments there is a voice inside which speaks and says, 'This is the real me!'"[2]

The phrase "a subjective sense" states that identity begins with the inner disposition. That is one decisive clue to the kinship between the language of identity and of Christian spirituality. Jesus' insistence upon the interior quality of human response to God finds crowning expression in his statement, "Blessed are the pure in heart, for they shall see God" (Matt. 5:8). Paul and John are at one in stressing the inner quality of the Christian life, as in the respective ways they speak of prayer, rebirth, love, faith, and hope. Nor do other authors depart from them. In a lovely manner this inwardness finds summation in the letter of James: "Is any one among you suffering? Let him pray. Is any cheerful? Let him sing praise" (James 5:13). The first elemental requirement of Christian identity is not assent to doctrine or even church attendance but rather a penetrating, subjective sense, a disposition of the heart.

One must go on to ask, A subjective sense of what? Erikson's answer is found in his second point: a sense of an invigorating sameness and continuity. That is not, one notes in passing, a boring, confining, stultifying sameness but an invigorating one. The subjective sense invigorates, but it does not produce discontinuity, a disjunction in the self. One quickly asks, Does the language here not depart from Christian experience? Does Christian experience of conversion, of being reborn, not entail a radical break with the past? In one sense it clearly does, but not in another sense. Saul of Tarsus was known to Paul the apostle. He recognized his same self, and he knew he possessed a continuity in self-consciousness. Is there invigoration in the subjective sense for Paul? The apostle's life testifies that there is, but the invigoration of his subjective sense went beyond his activism. "I press on," he wrote, "toward the goal for the prize of the upward call of God in Christ Jesus" (Phil. 3:14). Similarly, the Word which came to the leaders of Israel and to the people themselves invigorated them, produced a tradition which lived in their hearts, and over and over again not only renewed that tradition but also developed it. Jesus fulfilled the law and the prophets; he accomplished a transformation of the ancient tradition, but he did not break it. Indeed, one of the greatest continuities of Scripture is (1) the subjective sense of (2) an invigorating sameness which it exhibits and which it inspires.

The third point, namely, self-discovery, appears in the William James letter from which Erikson quotes. Erikson draws attention to the importance of feeling "most deeply and intensely alive. . . . *This* is the real me!'" Taken with the seriousness with which it is written, this element of the description signifies true self-discovery in secular, theoretical terms. Christian experience, on the other hand, sees self-discovery in theological terms. "Jesus answered him, 'Truly, truly, I

say to you, unless one is born anew, he cannot see the kingdom of God.'
. . . Do not marvel that I said to you, 'You must be born anew.' The wind
blows where it wills, and you hear the sound of it, but you do not know
whence it comes or whither it goes; so it is with every one who is born
of the Spirit" (John 3:3, 7–8). From the standpoint of the person,
Jesus' words suggest a form of self-discovery that reaches so deeply
into the consciousness that it must be described in primal terms. Only
the analogy of birth is adequate to describe it. One also recalls the Old
Testament and the primal nature of the new status and calling that
was given to the prophets, expressed by references to the womb (Jer.
1:5, also Isa. 49:1; Hos. 12:2–5). According to Jesus' startling words,
this "new me" is brought to birth by the Spirit of God, which touches
one like the wind blows, without one's knowing precisely how. After-
wards one might say that "it came upon me."

Both human identity and personal identity in Christ (1) include a
subjective sense; (2) produce an awareness of invigorating continuity;
and (3) yield a moment of feeling intensely alive, of discovery of the
"real me." At the same time this moment (4) cannot be protected by
any form of guarantee. Indeed, as soon as one tries to manufacture a
guarantee that an awareness of identity will continue, awareness
disappears. The discovery of the "real me" always includes:

> . . . an element of active tension, of holding my own as it were, and
> trusting outward things to perform their part so as to make it a full
> harmony, but without any guaranty that they will. Make it a guaranty . . .
> and the attitude immediately becomes to my consciousness stagnant and
> stingless. Take away the guaranty, and I feel (provided I am *ueberhaupt* in
> vigorous condition) a sort of deep enthusiastic bliss, of bitter willingness
> to do and suffer anything . . . and which, although it is a mere mood or
> emotion to which I can give no form in words, authenticates itself to me as
> the deepest principle of all active and theoretic determination which I
> possess . . .[3]

A striking kinship connects this passage to a pivotal aspect of the
fourth and fifth chapters of Paul's epistle to the Romans. There, Paul
insists that there is no guarantee, no justification for the person save
that provided by faith itself. When faith in the sense of commitment,
belief, and supreme trust is present, there is peace with God.[4] This
peace itself carries consequences of the hope of glory, of rejoicing in

suffering, and of the authentication of the whole provided by God's love in the heart. The apostle wrote:

> Therefore, since we are justified by faith, we have peace with God through our Lord Jesus Christ. Through him we have obtained access to this grace in which we stand, and we rejoice in our hope of sharing the glory of God. More than that, we rejoice in our sufferings, knowing that suffering produces endurance, and endurance produces character, and character produces hope, and hope does not disappoint us, because God's love has been poured into our hearts through the Holy Spirit which has been given to us. (Rom. 5:1–5)

These lines, like the chapters of which they are a part, do not treat Christian spirituality and the life in Christ from a psychological standpoint, and they should not be psychologized.[5] That, however, makes them more meaningful, for they clearly illumine what we have described as an identity in Christ. They do this in their insistence that there is no guarantee for identity save that provided by trust in the access that Christ gives us to God's grace.

So far, the aspects of human identity under consideration are the foundation stones of the structure of identity. There is no sense of identity, Christian or otherwise, unless there be (1) a subjective, inner sense; (2) an invigorated continuity of the self; (3) true self-discovery; and (4) the recognition that this cannot be manufactured or guaranteed in any way save by active trust. These elements, however, are put together through (5) a lifelong process that unites two fundamental aspects of human existence:

> . . . we deal with a process "located" in the *core of the individual* and yet also *in the core of his communal culture*, a process which establishes, in fact, the identity of those two identities. . . . And finally, in discussing identity, as we now see, we cannot separate personal growth and communal change, nor can we separate . . . the identity crisis in individual life and contemporary crisis in historical development because the two help to define each other and are truly relative to each other. In fact, the whole interplay between the psychological and the social, the developmental and the historical, for which identity formation is of prototypal significance, could be conceptualized only as a kind of *psychosocial relativity*.[6]

Stressing the interplay between the psychological and the social, Erikson remarks that the growth and formation of personal identity has prototypal significance. The psychological and the social come together in the long process of forming a personal identity; this process therefore becomes a prototype of the intimate interplay between the psychological and the social in human experience. When there is "identity of those two identities," in other words, when the psychological and the social come together, the process of forming a personal identity takes place. When, however, the psychological and the social are out of gear, difficulties and crises in forming personal identity occur.

We have sought, by means of tracing a certain complementarity between scriptural thought and Erikson's thought, to illumine one aspect of Christian spirituality: the shift in personal identity that occurs when a person moves from an orientation in one of the world's peoples to an orientation in the people of God. What has thus far been said may be clarified further by indicating three consequences of this aspect of Christian spirituality.

First, as a process of forming personal identity in Christ, Christian spirituality is to be carefully distinguished from the observances inherent in the traditions of Christianity. By "observances" we mean the repeated acknowledgments of belief in the creeds, the following of accepted moral laws, codes, or principles, participation in liturgies, whether public or private, the fulfillment of churchly institutional requirements, and other similar aspects of the accumulated traditions of the various churches. These observances, generally speaking, have intrinsic and thus necessary value: history does not know of a church or a community of Christians that can exist without some measure of observance. At the same time, the performance of these observances, however faithfully and correctly done, is not a substitute for the process of forming a personal identity in Christ. Few, one suspects, would maintain that it is. The difficulty arises when it is recognized that these observances themselves are a part of and a contribution to the nurturing of Christian identity. Observances then frequently become a substitute for Christian identity instead of remaining only a help.

The crossover from observance-as-help to observance-as-substitute is subtle but devastating. When relying upon observance, whether by conviction or inadvertence, one runs the danger of seeking a guarantee for the new sense of identity in Christ. When observances are turned into guaranties, the invigorating life with God recedes, losing its power. Observances in themselves do not produce either a subjective sense or a merging of the inner nature of the person with the communal. Observances, however, help when they lead to repeated exposure of the self to God-in-Christ at the boundary of life, when they lead, that is, to the new identity found in the people of God. Then a further dimension is added.

The second consequence of a personal identity in Christ concerns the relationship, which we have previously noted, between the psychological and the social aspects of life. This relationship is a critical spiritual issue of our time. On the one hand, it is no accident that current society exhibits overweening tendencies to psychologize life. These tendencies result far less from the communications skills of the psychologist and the pseudopsychologists than from universal experience of the inner conditions of the spirit. We all experience life torn from within by psychological forces of awesome power. If it doesn't happen personally to us, we see it happen to a family member or to the person next door. On the other hand, society itself offers little stability within which to work out the urgent problems of the spirit. So much evidence appears daily that Western civilization is in serious trouble that explicit statements, from presidents on down, seem necessary to assure us it is not so. Many issues—the bomb, energy, pollution, population, the dollar—cause an ultimate fear for either our way of life or for life itself. Indeed, the capacity of single issues to render plausible visions of Armageddon is one of the distinguishing marks of our century. Society batters the individual with both present disruptions and all-too-real fears of future disaster. The inner forces and the social powers are equally serious, and together they appear worse because they appear to be unrelated. Although many strive to make things better—now seeking personal adjustment, now hoping for social corrections or reforms—the gap between the psychological and the social, the inner and the environmental, seems to be all-but-unbridgeable. The spiritual issue therefore is: Are the psychological and the social related, and, if they are, how does this relationship occur?

In reply, we recall our main thesis: the destinies of the person and the people are fundamentally intertwined. Moreover, the mutual relationship between the peoplehood and the person is the point or realm at which healing power enters. In Erikson's terms this healing is the formation of the "real me" which springs from the psycho-social relationship. In scriptural terms this healing is the result of God's presence, everywhere creating and re-creating peoplehood and the identity of persons within peoplehood, always active and alive. Thus one is led not to a gap between the psychological and the social but to a unity of them. This is, of course, not always the way these matters are viewed. Frequently, one of two extremes is argued. On the one hand, our individualistic culture traditionally maintains that society is made up of individuals, and that the moral quality of individuals determines the moral quality of society. Thus Christians have felt that if society were peopled by good Christians or by good individuals who live according to Christian moral standards, all would be well or, at least, better. On the other hand, the other extreme—that the structure or system of society has preponderant influence not only upon the moral quality of society but also upon the moral quality of the individuals within it—has long been advanced. Surely truths that shouldn't be dismissed exist on both sides of this familiar discussion. Difficulties come from its either/or aspect. Human beings are not doomed to endure the consequences of a great gap between the inner and the outer, the psychological and the social, the individual and the structural. Rather, the person exists within the people and the people within the person. One cannot say that people is prior to person or that person is prior to people. Scriptural perspectives perceive that these two form a fundamental unity, and that this unity is subject to the graciousness of God.

This view of Christian spirituality yields a third consequence. The proof of the whole lies in the transformation of the old by the new. Scripture testifies that God does not leave us in the penultimate world of peoples where human identities are formed and lived out as best as possible. Hope lies in the final establishment of the kingdom of God. Thus Christian spirituality not only knows identity formation, but it also knows redemption, the redemption of peoplehood by peoplehood. If we cannot exist save by virtue of peoplehood, and if we are captive to its limitations, then redemption comes by a new peoplehood. That does not imply a replacement of one peoplehood by the other. It does not signify the existence of a religious people alongside others. It does not evoke competition as when empires compete with other empires. The redemption of peoplehood is instead brought about by transformation.

Paul states it clearly when describing the church to the Romans: "Do not be conformed to this world but be transformed by the renewal of your mind, that you may prove what is the will of God, what is good and acceptable and perfect" (Rom. 12:2). The phrase "this world" or, as in the Greek, "this age" may mean the specific world or age of ancient Rome or the generalized world of all peoples. In any case, redemption consists in transforming the bond which unites any—and, ultimately, all—of the peoples of the world. That redemption begins within the current life of the world's peoples, and it is validated or, in Paul's language, "proved" by doing the will of God. That proof, however, begins and has its roots in the "renewal of your mind." Paul used comparable language to the Philippians, exhorting them to "have this mind among yourselves, which you have in Christ Jesus" (Phil. 2:5). Transformation results from this juxtaposition of the "mind" of Christ's people with the peoples of this age. Such a transformation is possible in life because of Christ's power to lead a person to God, to introduce a person to the clarity of God, and, at the same time, to make the mystery of God known to the person. Yet transformation takes place because a people exists for which Christ supplies the uniting bond, and it takes place within that people. Redemption thus comes to the person because a new peoplehood is offered and entered. The evidence that this redemption is real lies in the transformation of the person's identity, in the shift from being oriented in one of the peoples of this age to being oriented in the people belonging to the age and the future inaugurated by Christ.

9

The Enduring Problem and Strength of Christian Spirituality

If one is a Christian, what occupies the attention of heart, soul, and mind? What is the temper or texture of life?

Christian spirituality goes to the root. It consists of a shift in one's own personal sense of identity brought about by moving from one peoplehood to another. It begins to take place because at some point, by some means, a Christian has an unmistakable sense of something beyond; there is glimpse of hope, the tremor of a new power, an inner feeling of something happening that is quite different from other things that happen. Above all, there is a strange, comforting, exciting, somewhat apprehensive perception of not being alone. These motions of the heart do not remove the processes or problems of everyday life; they put this stream of living into a new environment. But they do affect life because they are motions at the origin and root of sustenance that transform the way a person lives. From the innermost parts, a Christian knows the capacity of God to transform a previous identity into one that aspires to the mind and stature of Christ.

Transformation consumes heart, soul, and mind. The strength of Christian spirituality goes hand in hand with its basic problem: the temper or texture of Christian living consists of tension—the outer tension between the kingdom of God and the peoplehood of one's birth and the inner tension as a new personal identity transforms the old. The natural human tendency is stubbornly to resist tension, either by rejecting it outright or, when in a Christianized civilization, by downplaying it, accommodating the mystery and clarity of God's kingdom to an inherited mixture of accepted values. The enduring problem of Christian spirituality is to maintain the tension; likewise, the strength

64

of Christian spirituality is its capacity to restore and maintain the tension in its true form. The problem is vividly stated by Richard Niebuhr:

> We look back longingly at times to some past age when, we think, confidence in the One God was the pervasive faith of men; for instance, to early Christianity, or to the church society of the Middle Ages, or to early Protestantism, or to Puritan New England, or to the pious nineteenth century. But when we study these periods we invariably find in them a mixture of the faith in the One God with social faith and polytheism; and when we examine our longings we often discover that what we yearn for is the security of the closed society with its social confidence and social loyalty. It is very questionable, despite many protestations to the contrary, despite the prevalence of self-pity among some modern men because "God is dead," that anyone has ever yearned for radical faith in the One God.[1]

Niebuhr puts his finger upon one aspect of the matter in speaking of "the mixture of faith in the One God with social faith and polytheism." What might such a mixture look like? For an illustration, one may consider the meeting, in the closing years of the nineteenth century, between President McKinley and a group of his Methodist friends about his decision to send Americans to "civilize" the Philippines. He said to them:

> I am not ashamed to tell you, gentlemen, that I went down on my knees and prayed Almighty God for light and guidance more than one night. And one night late it come to me this way. . . . There was nothing left for us to do but take them all and to educate the Filipinos and uplift and civilize and Christianize them, and by God's grace do the very best we could by them, as our fellow men for whom Christ died.[2]

McKinley's reasons for advancing upon the Philippines possess an innocence, but it is a terrible innocence. It comes from his inability to maintain the tension between his own civilization and the kingdom of God and from his assumption that by "civilizing" the Philippine population, the United States would be doing them a favor as "our fellow men for whom Christ died."

McKinley was not the only person with this idea. Josiah Strong, a Protestant minister of McKinley's time who was the general secretary of the Evangelical Alliance and had become a national figure of wide influence, had, if anything, a stronger view.

> It seems to me that God, with infinite wisdom and skill, is here training the

Anglo-Saxon race for an hour sure to come in the World's future. . . . The time is coming when the pressure of population on the means of subsistence will be felt here as it is now felt in Europe and Asia. . . . Then this race of unequalled energy, with all the majesty of numbers and the might of wealth behind it—the representative, let us hope, of the largest liberty, the purest Christianity, the highest civilization—having developed peculiarly aggressive traits calculated to impress its institutions upon mankind, will spread itself over the earth.[3]

In these statements one readily discerns a mixture of social faith and polytheism with faith in the One God. The positions of McKinley and Strong are not isolated: they reflect the America of which they were a part. The peoplehood of the United States had been long in formation, and it was composed of many elements. Fused in a historical experience that began in the early seventeenth century, it formed the nineteenth-century American civilization in which the idea of Manifest Destiny formed a strong, if not dominant, role. There was faith in the One God, as McKinley kneeling in prayer symbolized. Yet that faith was mixed with a social faith in which there was polytheism—the worship of gods in the form of elements that commanded American loyalty and unleashed American energy.

Niebuhr goes further, however, than historical analysis. He says that "when we examine our longings we often discover that what we yearn for is the security of the closed society with its social confidence and social loyalty." Today, the language of McKinley and Strong has changed, and many would reject the substance of what these representatives of state and church stood for. Wars, depressions, alienations, historical sophistication, revolts, the pressures of the world's peoples upon the United States, and fears for the future have replaced earlier simplicities. One result of these complex developments is a change in American identity, a shift away from the confidence of the nineteenth century toward a pluralism which, while undoubtedly beneficial, is also evidence of major change.

Even so, the underlying spirituality dies hard, both in the churches and in the nation as a whole. Religion generally and Christianity specifically continue to have an accepted place in society. Church is a part of the American way of life. In itself there is nothing wrong with that. Trouble arises, however, when church finds its principal meaning as being part of the American way of life. Many today, for instance, argue that to ensure the health and future of the nation, including its preeminent role in international affairs, the religious part of U.S. life needs revival. This attitude does not originate from the kingdom of God and its meaning for the United States but rather from a lament over the loss of the security of a past society supposedly better grounded in Christian values.

The mixture of faith in One God with other elements to form a U.S. civilization should never—not in the nineteenth century and not today—deflect attention from a fundamental point: whether or not ours be called a "Christian civilization," it is a peoplehood just like all the others that exist in the world today and have existed throughout history. Even though it has strong Christian elements within it, even though it behaves kindly toward Christianity and the church, it does not function as a rung on a ladder, or as a stage on the progressive way to the kingdom of God. It functions as a peoplehood and, as such, as a boundary or limit to the life of those within it. In Niebuhr's terms it is a closed society; similarly, in Scriptural terms it is a peoplehood, a provision of God, but a provision which functions to delineate the boundary at which people again and again encounter the graciousness of God.

The problem of Christian spirituality arises when the function of peoplehood is distorted. The problem is not simply wronghead-edness—McKinley's imperialism or Strong's racism, for instance. Christian spirituality is in trouble when the peoplehood has too high a value, when the American way of life invariably seems to many of us to be the best, and when, therefore, it becomes the standard by which God's will is understood and God's purpose is measured. When that happens it leads to feeling blessed and confirmed in all that one is and has been rather than to feeling compelled to seek a new kingdom. Furthermore, it is also likely to produce triumphalism and the urge to dominate others and the future.

The experience that flows from scriptural spirituality is different. It perceives that our peoplehood is valued and precious because it provides for our life in necessary but highly relative ways. It perceives that this peoplehood to which we belong is not some kind of approximation of the kingdom of God, but rather it is one of the fundamental conditions and limits of life at which we encounter God. Christian spirituality grows when the functions of peoplehood are not distorted but held in true relation to God. Christian spirituality is visible when it maintains the tension between the peoplehood that upholds our civilization and the peoplehood of God, available now and yet to come.

The strength of scriptural spirituality lies in its capacity to discern the right relation between one's peoplehood and the purpose of God. One might ask whether there is such a thing as a true orientation, whether evidence of genuine transformation exists, whether faith in God is a mere ideal, or whether it is expressed in the actual church and in the affairs of the nation. An adage from the time of the Reformation, that supposed golden age of Protestantism, had it that "true Christians are few and far between." Are there any people who discern the right relation between their own peoplehood and God's kingdom? The history of the church, past and present, shows that there are. Among them, perhaps no one has spoken more authentically than Abraham Lincoln, whose Second Inaugural Address is also a product of the nineteenth century:

> The Almighty has His own purposes. "Woe unto the world because of offenses! for it must needs be that offenses come; but woe to that man by whom the offense cometh." If we shall suppose that American slavery is one of those offenses which, in the providence of God, must needs come, but which, having continued through His appointed time, He now wills to remove, and that He gives to both North and South this terrible war, as the woe due to those by whom the offense came, shall we discern therein any departure from those Divine attributes which the believers in the living God always ascribe to Him? Fondly do we hope—fervently do we pray— that this mighty scourge of war may speedily pass away. Yet, if God will that it continue until all the wealth piled by the bondsman's two hundred and fifty years of unrequited toil shall be sunk, and until every drop of blood drawn with the lash shall be paid by another drawn with the sword, as was said three thousand years ago, so still it must be said, "The judgments of the Lord are true and righteous altogether."
>
> With malice toward none; with charity for all; with firmness in the right as God gives us to see the right, let us strive on to finish the work we are in; to bind up the nation's wounds; to care for him who shall have borne the battle, and for his widow, and his orphan; to do all which may achieve and cherish a just and lasting peace among ourselves and with all nations.[4]

Unlike his successors later in the nineteenth century, Lincoln did not read the language of God as if it were the language of American civilization. Even though his address shows the marks of its time, place, and people, it portrays the tragedy of America in 1865 in the light of the righteousness of God. Of Lincoln, the historian Allan Nevins wrote: "A religious feeling as to the import of the War grew upon him. It was, he thought, a testing by God of the purposes and devotion of the American people, a punishment by God for their past errors and an opportunity given them by God to re-create their life in a nobler pattern. In his daily work, Lincoln could be very hardheaded, stern, and even relentless. But he had a vision, and little by little he strove to lift the people to it."[5] One does not doubt the sincerity of McKinley and Strong and their successors even in the present, but one notes that for people like them no tension results from being both an American and a Christian. For Lincoln, however, the inherent tension between God and a people was a driving power.

The paragraph by Richard Niebuhr quoted earlier concludes with a strange sentence. "It is very questionable, despite many protestations to the contrary, despite the prevalence of self-pity among some modern men because 'God is dead,' that anyone has ever yearned for radical faith in the One God." That statement can scarcely intend to present a conclusion from observed fact. It expresses, rather, the nature and tension of Christian spirituality. Yearning is a disposition of human love and desire. Yearning is fulfilled if we get what we yearn for, and one is likely to judge fulfillment according to some line or curve of progress. Scripture, however, describes the spiritual life differently; yearnings may be fulfilled, but not in the way those yearnings lead us to expect. Christian spirituality begins when God meets us at the boundaries of all our yearnings, or at the boundaries of all of our disappointments in them.

Christian spirituality does not flow from a familiar societal environment, from a hallowed church culture, or from a mixture of the two. It springs from a different homeland, a new peoplehood, a universal kingdom. One does not yearn for that; it comes upon one from beyond the limits of human experience. Christian spirituality, moreover, proceeds on a different plane than one that can be measured by the progressive fulfillment of our yearnings. Life with God-in-Christ puts one on a plane of trust that the kingdom beyond history redeems the peoples of history. One does not yearn for that; one is seized by it. The primary movement of Christian spirituality is neither backward to a supposed security nor forward to one imagined, but rather it is a movement of transition from a peoplehood of human necessity to the peoplehood of God's purpose, a transition marked by the transformation of one's very sense of identity. One does not yearn for that, for it is accomplished by a faith that gives security only in the measure that risk is taken. When, however, this gift is given, when the different homeland is no longer strange, and when the inner parts are invigorated by their transformation and the tension that results, the yearning finds fulfillment, because it, too, has been transformed. It is then a yearning for God, for the people of God, and for the purposes of God among the peoples of the world.

Part III

SPIRITUALITY AMID THE LOST

The axis of biblical spirituality turns on more than God's relation to peoples and persons. The knowledge of God given to Israel and then to the church yielded further knowledge of humanity. Biblical experience went beyond the significance of peoples and persons to other constant elements of life. These elements are themselves boundaries. In their respective yet interlocking ways they hold human beings captive, either in subtle ways that make captivity seem attractive or in gross forms that create turbulence and trouble.

The theme of this part is that Scripture speaks of three elements of life that are boundaries; that the sense of being lost in life derives from the effect of these limits upon peoples and persons; and that knowing "a way home" yields a further aspect of spirituality: participation in the new world of Christ.

10

Sin: A Compulsion in the Mask of Freedom

A central theme of Scripture is that without God we are lost.

> Out of the depths I cry to thee, O Lord!
> Lord, hear my voice!
> Let thy ears be attentive to the voice of my supplications! (Ps. 130:1–2)

This psalm of worship before God is not alone in registering the perception that without God we are lost. Scripture's presentation of history—some of it, as Walter Harrelson notes[1] of the books of Samuel, "the best historical writing known from the ancient world"—was obviously not written simply in order to record Israel's past. History recorded in the Bible has a further purpose; it contains a dual theme that stresses the fear or fact of Israel's being lost and deprived of peoplehood, identity, and future, while it affirms that this deprivation is overcome by knowledge of God's presence and purpose.

Expressed in various moods and manners, this theme comes to concern more than Israel. A disclosure unfolds: the human feeling of being lost is neither a periodic moodiness nor a permanent condition; it is the situation of human beings who cut themselves off from God. Scripture, however, does not leave the matter at that. The scriptural writers had a definite understanding of human lostness, derived from their knowledge of God. Speaking of the account of Christ in the first verses of John's Gospel, Edwyn Hoskins wrote: "When this Life is recognized and accepted, it is Light; for Light is the manifestation of Life. But the proper sphere of light is darkness. Light does not avoid the darkness: it shines in it."[2] In the presence of God three dimensions of the darkness, three constant conditions of human life, become clear. All human beings: (1) are unavoidably subject to a corrupting, inner compulsion which puts severe limits upon human freedom; (2) participate in large-scale structures of life which have the effect of giving power to human achievement and order in human life, but also dominate and alienate human identity; (3) are actually dependent, yet strive to achieve an illusory independence and autonomy. Each of these dimensions powerfully—fatefully—affects peoples and peoplehood. We shall turn to the first dimension in the remainder of this chapter; in chapters 11 and 12 we will examine the second and third. Chapters 13, 14, and 15 will discuss the significance of each dimension for spirituality.

A COMPULSION

Scripture minces no words when it names sin:

Nathan said to David, "You are the man. . . . You have smitten Uriah the Hittite with the sword, and have taken his wife to be your wife, and have slain him with the sword of the Ammonites." (2 Sam. 12:7, 9)

There is no faithfulness or kindness,
    and no knowledge of God in the land;
there is swearing, lying, killing, stealing, and committing adultery;
    they break all bounds and murder follows murder. (Hos. 4:1-2)

" . . . because they carried into exile a whole people . . .
because they have ripped up women with child . . .
because they sell the righteous for silver,
    and the needy for a pair of shoes—
they that trample the head of the poor into the dust of the earth,
    and turn aside the way of the afflicted;
a man and his father go in to the same maiden,
    so that my holy name is profaned. . . .
They do not know how to do right," says the Lord,
"those who store up violence and robbery in their strongholds. . . .
who oppress the poor, who crush the needy . . ."
(Amos 1:6, 13; 2:6-7; 3:10; 4:1)

For they eat the bread of wickedness
    and drink the wine of violence. (Prov. 4:17)

Diagnosing human evil, Paul quickly becomes specific. The end of the first chapter of Romans includes a concrete description of what he means by a "base mind and improper conduct":

They were filled with all manner of wickedness, evil, covetousness, malice. Full of envy, murder, strife, deceit, malignity, they are gossips, slanderers, haters of God, insolent, haughty, boastful, inventors of evil, disobedient to parents, foolish, faithless, heartless, ruthless. (Rom. 1:29–31)

The list has force not only because it names specific evils but because these suggest something else. When any of the evils appears, whether in the inner spaces of the mind or in the outer spaces of conduct, sin is there. These evils point beyond themselves.

If one asks, To what do these evils point? If these be sins, what is sin? one has, biblically speaking, started on the right road. That is the way Israel's experience went. To be led out of Egyptian captivity, to receive the revelation of the will of God in the commandments, to disobey again and again, and then repeatedly to experience the unmistakable graciousness of God—all of this could scarcely let Israel's leaders and people rest content. The authors of Scripture were varied. Many were people who, especially in worship, maintained the traditions by repeating them word-of-mouth; others gathered these traditions, edited them, and put them down in writing. There were people of different gifts and interests—historians, poets, preachers, theologians, prophets, dramatists, lovers of divine wisdom—yet they were united by a passionate knowledge of God that they recognized as having been given to them. They were participants who knew the curse and the blessing, the darkness and the light. Their participation enabled them to know the darkness because of the light, to enter the interior of the human condition itself. What was wrong?

Various terms describe the process of continually falling short and then turning away: "missing the mark," "making a mistake," "rebelling," "going astray," "engaging in abnormal legal, moral, or religious behavior." Through experience all these descriptions were understood to have common elements.[3] "Sin" became a general term that gathered specific sins together, providing further meaning to them all. The vast contrast between the light of God and the darkness of life was measured not only by the single acts that humans perform but by sin, a condition of human life itself. In this sense, sin has two related aspects.

The first aspect of sin is suggested by the modern word "compulsion." Frequently used in current culture, the word deserves a pause to recall its meaning. In the psychological sense, compulsion means "a strong, usually irresistible impulse to perform an act that is contrary to the will of the subject" (*Random House Dictionary*). One of the classic scriptural texts about sin says much the same thing:

> I do not understand my own actions. For I do not do what I want, but I do the very thing I hate. Now if I do what I do not want, I agree that the law is good. So then it is no longer I that do it, but sin which dwells within me. For I know that nothing good dwells within me, that is, in my flesh. I can will what is right, but I cannot do it. For I do not do the good I want, but the evil I do not want is what I do. Now if I do what I do not want, it is no longer I that do it, but sin which dwells within me. (Rom. 7:15–20)

When, in the year that King Uzziah died, Isaiah stood in the presence of the Lord, perceived that he was unclean, and cried: "Woe is me!" Paul's cry is similar: "Wretched man that I am!" (Rom. 7:24). With a clarity not hitherto articulated, Paul perceived that the human condition of being lost, of being without God, comes about by an inner power, a compulsion: sin. That leads to the other aspect of sin. If sin is a compulsion, the second aspect of sin is discovered by inquiring, A compulsion to do what?

What happened in Eden between the male, the female, and God? In reply, one may think of the serpent, an unforgettable figure, a symbol—at least—of the aspect of sin that is not simply "I," and reflect that the woman and the man were tempted. One may think of the nakedness, the self-consciousness, the fear and shame, the lost innocence, the dissonance, and the guilt, feeling their elemental reverberations in one's own consciousness. The temptation and its result point to the center: the two ate "of the tree of the knowledge of good and evil" (Gen. 2:17). That was the act. The meaning of it is not appreciated save as the serpent's comment "You will be like God, knowing good and evil" is understood (Gen. 3:5). At first sight the phrase is puzzling; we are, after all, supposed to know good and evil in their moral sense. As used by the serpent, however, these terms do not refer primarily, or even at all, to moral knowledge. They are a manner of speaking and mean simply "everything" or, when used in the negative, "nothing," as when Moses told the people that they would not enter the promised land until the children, "who this day have no knowledge of good or evil," could possess it (Deut. 1:39). If Israel's children were on that day babies who knew nothing, Adam and Eve ate of that which they thought would give them knowledge of everything, a real omniscience. Moreover, "knowing" meant more than an intellectual enterprise; it connoted going deeper, to an experiencing, as when in the sexual act men and women "know" each other. "Knowing" meant also being able, having an ability to accomplish. The momentous act penetrated to these realms, disclosing their portent. Humans would know the corrupting power of hubris, the attractiveness of the urge to attain God-like knowledge, experience, and ability.[4]

The symbolism that introduces us to these realms of Adam and Eve is neither a literal account nor a flight of the imagination. Paul Ricoeur speaks of "a great discovery: the discovery of the *symbolic* function of the myth. . . . But then we should not say, 'The story of the "fall" is *only* a myth'—that is to say, something less than history—but 'The story of the fall has the greatness of myth'—that is to say, has more meaning than a true history."[5] By "a true history" Ricoeur means an account "coordinated with the time of history and the space of geography."[6] The symbolism of Genesis 3, freed from the confines of particular time and space, nevertheless expresses history, the history of Israel's struggle with God and of the self-knowledge that resulted from it. That struggle was decisive. To Israel it yielded knowledge of a fundamental fact of human life: the human being is possessed of a compulsive tendency to rebel, to usurp the role of God.

A succinct sentence by Paul states what this entails. Speaking of people in general, Paul wrote: "they exchanged the truth about God for a lie and worshiped and served the creature rather than the Creator, who is blessed for ever" (Rom. 1:24). This sentence occurs in the midst of an analysis of the root nature of human ills and evils in which Paul maintains that truth is suppressed by wickedness. Reading this, one is brought up short. Our culture does not readily find wickedness to be the main enemy of truth in the way that Paul does. In accord with our heritage from ancient Greece and the eighteenth-century Enlightenment, we assume that truth is opposed, suppressed, or hidden by ignorance and error. This assumption allows us to define wickedness largely as error or mistake, thus differing from Scripture. Paul and Scripture as a whole do include error and mistake in wickedness, but they insist that wickedness goes beyond them and that it forms the real opposition to truth. So wickedness, not ignorance or error is, in biblical thought, the principal opponent of truth.

The wicked person is one who worships the creature rather than the Creator. That is what Jeremiah had in mind when he reported that the Lord said that the people "have forsaken me . . . and hewed out cisterns for themselves" (2:13). Doing this is idolatry, always and everywhere Scripture's "Enemy Number One" (see chapter 5). In its most comprehensive form idolatry is the act of worshiping the creature, any creature, rather than the Creator. At this level idolatry does not apply simply to the religious side of life. It is endemic to human existence—explosive, corrupting, and dangerous for one's relationship to self, neighbor, world, and God.

Specific instances abound in Scripture that illustrate the principle of idolatry. We choose three: achievement, self-saving, and the troubled psyche.

ACHIEVEMENT

Then they said, "Come, let us build ourselves a city, and a tower with its top in the heavens, and let us make a name for ourselves, lest we be scattered abroad upon the face of the whole earth." (Gen. 11:4)

The account of the Tower of Babel concentrates upon a vast area of human endeavor. It speaks of corporate achievement in which individuals play their respective roles. The story concerns achievement that aims too high for a purpose that is too self-centered, and it makes two points concerning it: (1) The realm of corporate achievement is not exempt from self-deification. The exaltation of the self is not merely done by the individual, and it is not merely a matter of inner spirituality. Communal, corporate life also engages in idolatry. (2) The overtones of the Tower of Babel story and the placement of it in primeval history imply that self-exaltation not only accompanies human social achievement but is endemic to it. No group is exempt, as all history, including American history, confirms. Idolatry in this realm is neither rare nor accidental.

Amos and the prophets who followed him perceived the power of communal, endemic idolatry. These men heard God and confronted Israel in the same basic terms. By the time of David and Solomon, Israel had come a long way from the tribes which had wandered in the desert. The monarchy was a time of acknowledged greatness for

Israel. By the eighth century B.C., however, grave political, economic, and international difficulties had overtaken the nation. Israel's peoplehood, and with it the nation's creativity and character, had become corrupt to the point of danger. In response, the prophets did not stir the fires of reaction and seek to restore Israel's former political and cultural glory, advocating an even greater civilization, a "Number One People" chosen by God. They perceived that pretension of that sort, and confidence in the alliances and armaments necessary to support it, constituted the wrong course to take (Isa. 31:1). Instead, the prophets captured the true meaning of the monarchy. They sought in the name of God to reverse Israel's self-consciousness, insisting upon a peoplehood in which creativity and character were founded upon the righteousness, the justice, of God. In their thought Israel would not build to reach the heavens. Instead, Israel would be known as the servant of God, the light to the nations (Isa. 49:1–13).

The timeless story of Babel expresses that epoch-making work of the eighth-century prophets of Israel; both story and prophets perceive that peoples and peoplehood are afflicted with tragedy and that collective, corporate life contains the seeds of its own corruption. Achievement that exalts itself, reaching to the heavens by trusting its own devices, is a vigorous form of worshiping the creature.

SELF-SAVING

As achievement is an extroverted form of creature worship, self-preoccupation is an introverted form. "For whoever would save his life will lose it, and whoever loses his life for my sake and the gospel's will save it" (Mark 8:35). One side of Jesus' extraordinary paradox, enunciated when he first forecast his death and laid down the conditions of discipleship, brings immediately to mind the many self-obsessed defensive, clinging moods and strategies that arise in our hearts and are played out in speech and action in order to "save" our lives. Jesus' few words make us aware that it is human to try to save our lives by any plausible means that are accessible. The other side of the paradox, "whoever loses his life . . . ," a process elsewhere called "self-emptying" (Phil. 2:7), stirs up hesitation, resistance, and fear. At once we become aware that the idea of losing our lives renders us too vulnerable, too greatly subject to what we cannot control, and is therefore fearsome. The fear of the risk and vulnerablility incurred in losing our lives reinforces our preoccupation with saving them. This circle of fear and defensive self-preoccupation forms the target of Jesus' paradox, which is both attack and revelation. By attacking the action of putting self in the center, the paradox triggers our minds to perceive the many ways in which humans are preoccupied with self.

THE TROUBLED PSYCHE

Now the works of the flesh are plain: immorality, impurity, licentiousness, idolatry, sorcery, enmity, strife, jealousy, anger, selfishness, dissension, party spirit, envy, drunkenness, carousing, and the like. (Gal. 5:19–21)

Self-preoccupation is taken further by Paul in the above list, not unlike the passage from Romans quoted earlier in this chapter. This time, however, Paul has given the list a title: "the works of the flesh." This list is introduced in Galatians by a reference to the "desires of the flesh." Paul is not referring to an urge to sojourn among the fleshpots, at least not in the first instance, but to life as it is when sin is in control.[7]

Personally, I have to confess that when I read these verses—as I once did—as a list of naughty, immoral things I should not do (which, of course, it is), I remained untouched. From this viewpoint I could quickly say that I was not guilty of some of these works. That led me then to a moral balancing act: if I was guilty of some works but innocent of others, then maybe I was getting by. Yet this did not help me with the uneasiness I felt when I read, for instance, the Sermon on the Mount and discovered that inner attitudes are what really count.

The discovery, however, that Paul's list and Jesus' teaching about inner attitudes come to the same thing opened up a new vista. The Sermon on the Mount and Paul's list both recognize the power of the troubled psyche, pointing to it rather than merely to immoral actions. Richard Sipe, a psychologist, was participating in a discussion about the meaning of faith in God. Restless, he broke forth, complaining that the discussion was proceeding as if those present "had God in their hand." "The average person struggles," he insisted. "We are all involved in a quest into the dark and elusive, almost unassailable fortress on the inside of human beings. This realm of the unconscious is peopled by the most primitive devils and the most unreligious impulses."[8] It goes too far to say that Paul's works of the flesh deal with the subconscious, but his treatment points to that inner, subterranean world. Works of the flesh do not result from a decision cooly made. Caught up in any one of them—like anger, for instance—one feels its driving impulse springing up from within, rising with frightening power. Even if anger is confined to thoughts or fantasy, it leaves behind the feeling of damage having been done to oneself; and, if the anger is acted out in speech or deed, damage is done to others as well. These works of the flesh belong to the self, and are a part of it, whether in fantasy, embryo, or action. These works are not just bad things. They result from "the most primitive devils and the most unreligious impulses" rising up from the depths. Jesus' paradox about saving and losing one's life, his stress upon inner dispositions, and Paul's naming of the works of the flesh all penetrate to the troubled psyche.[9]

From Adam and Eve to Paul, Scripture makes clear that the trouble of the psyche is universal. Observable not only in those who are psychotic, whose inner difficulty reaches a particular and extreme form, the troubled psyche is found in everyone. Moreover, in the view of Scripture, the psyche does not belong to some primitive state of humanity or of culture, to be outgrown as humanity, or a part of it, progresses. The trouble is endemic. To be human is to experience the troubled psyche.

Furthermore, this condition requires understanding at two levels: the immediate and the ultimate. From oppression in Egypt to the healings of Jesus, Scripture attests the concern of God for the immediate conditions of life. Among the conditions are the troubles of the self. Requiring attention, they are objects of God's love, whether they be the ravings of one possessed or the actions of a prodigal. From my own experience I know that there come moments when the all-important thing for one's spiritual life, for commitment to God, and for getting through the day, is some adjustment, some healing of the immediate inner conflict. At the same time, while that adjustment or healing is necessary, it is not salvation, as I knew even when psychotherapy produced some light at the end of a dark tunnel.

In the process of healing I understood afresh the second level, the ultimate level of understanding the troubled psyche. I discovered—as if it were new—that there is a basic pattern, a deep rhyme and reason behind psychic turmoil. The pattern consists of a crucial connection made by Scripture: that at root turmoils are caused by the inherent compulsion to worship the creature rather than the Creator. In my own case the creature was a set of values internalized from childhood in a particular way—values, as Jeremiah implied long ago, which had so taken hold that they commanded obedience and worship and later on wrought havoc.

The precise connection between immediate psychic turmoil and a compulsion to creature-worship may not be discerned easily. For me, one of the greatest contributions of psychological science has been in helping us discern this connection. Obviously, Scripture does not enter these diagnostic realms. It does, however, emphatically make the connection between psychic trouble and creature-worship, its ultimate cause. The connection between the two shows that the human is constituted so as to be subjected both to compulsion and to the troubles resulting from compulsion.

In our culture this is not an easy analysis to accept. It is grim and dark. Even so, I find it liberating. It tells me that those to whom God spoke stood as humans where I now stand. Their experiences bring aspects of personal and collective life into the open. I recognize those aspects as belonging to me; I know I cannot suppress them; and I know that I cannot either hide or run from them. Yet I am not trapped. God is present and speaks in this human situation. Moreover, I perceive a further aspect—that of the honor, dignity, and delicacy of the human constitution. The human creature is of such a wondrous texture that if worship is given to anything less then God, the human texture falls apart. Thus inner troubles are not inchoate. They have their own form and that form itself implies an ultimate remedy. If worshiping the creature is the diagnosis, worshiping the Creator is the cure. The problem is the perennial strength of the compulsion to do the one and not the other.

THE MASK OF FREEDOM

The compulsive, endemic nature of sin, whether exhibited in achievement, self-centeredness, or a troubled psyche, makes one ask, What about freedom? Usually, one thinks of freedom as freedom of choice, a subject on which Scripture is largely silent, but which it seems to assume as a normal part of life. Unlike metaphysics or social theory in this respect, Scripture is little, if at all, concerned with freedom as opposed to determinism, being free to choose as opposed to being a pawn in some larger scheme of things. In another sense, however, the scriptural analysis of sin has everything to do with freedom.

Sin is present not only in the choices made but in the very act of choosing. Thus I exercise freedom in choosing what I will do without realizing that in another, deeper sense I am not free. Underneath these choices the compulsion to self-worship or to the worship of other creatures operates so naturally, so much as a part of me, that I am scarcely aware of it. Even when I am aware I cannot get free from its subtlety and power. A captivity is at work. My freedom to do this or that is not a true freedom, but only an apparent one. At root the problem of human freedom is not the misuse of freedom of choice, important though that is. The problem is that I cannot get free from the compulsion to worship the creature, though I am free to decide the area or act in which that worship takes place. It is perhaps the final darkness, the ultimate lostness, that, until I am aware of sin, I believe myself to be free when in fact I am captive. In Romans, Paul asks: "Who will deliver me from this body of death?" (7:24). In Galatians he affirms with exultation: "For freedom Christ has set us free" (5:1). We are set free not simply to choose. We are set free from a slavery which is part of our being lost.

11

Powers: Domination in the Guise of Empowerment

A strong and experienced swimmer stood on a Connecticut beach. The breakers were running high. He dived into a great wave and emerged with a broken back and paralyzed legs. He had misjudged the undertow.

When Western civilization was animated by the spirit of the modern age, with scarcely any to question it, the tide of human history seemed to be running invincibly high. Human capacities and the ability to develop them appeared to be unlimited, especially with the great tool of science in hand, giving the age an atmosphere of confidence. That confidence was aggressive; energy abounded to create, to explore, and to conquer. Progress was either apparent or just around the corner on all fronts. The power of achievement exhilarated people and reached fabled heights. In this spirit, people felt and exercised their freedom. This spirit dominated whole peoples for two centuries.

In the 1930s, at the very center of the civilization which had been brought into being by the spirit of the modern age, the Nazi state arose and flourished for some ten years. Those who comprised it had many of the qualities of the modern spirit. They saw themselves as the tide of human history, running invincibly high. They had confidence in human capacities and used science better than most. They were aggressive in their confidence and had incredible energy. They were exhilarated by the power of achievement, felt themselves to be free, and gave a sense of freedom to millions in Germany. Even so, in spite of a few who admired them, they aroused fear and then hatred among the other nations who shared the same modern spirit. The Nazis were brought down. They had misjudged the undertow of history.

Scripture describes the undertow of history with picturesque language. The great statement about human sin and God's salvation from sin that occupies the first eight chapters of Romans concludes with a summary:

> For I am sure that neither death, nor life, nor angels, nor principalities, nor things present, nor things to come, nor powers, nor height, nor depth, nor anything else in all creation, will be able to separate us from the love of God in Christ Jesus our Lord. (Rom. 8:38–39)

Here, recognizable but remarkably different entities are somewhat surprisingly listed together, along with a reference to everything in "all creation." The assurance that these entities cannot separate us from the love of God in Christ clearly implies that, in effect, they try to do so. What specifically are these entities? How can such a passage be read and understood?[1]

A first way to read the passage is as a poetic affirmation that God's love in Christ is not defeated by anything. There are times, perhaps most of the time, when one does not want to analyze the passage but only give thanks, expressing confidence and taking courage from the fact that nothing can separate us from God's love in Christ.

A second way to read the passage is somewhat more reflective, and it is concerned with the apostle Paul himself. In the passage Paul affirms that God's love in Christ is not defeated by anything he encountered in the ancient Jewish and Greek worlds or by anything people in the ancient world felt to be real. This is a help for us because from this it is but a step to asking, Was that world so different from ours, after all, concerning death and things present and yet to come? The passage is written in language alien to our ears, but does that invalidate its meaning? Gordon Rupp has an interesting comment on the tendency to throw out ancient language too readily:

> Modern man smiles at the old Cornish prayer:
> From Ghoulies and Ghostlies, and long-leggity Beasties
> And all Things that go bump in the Night,
> Good Lord deliver us.
>
> . . . And as one who lived as a Methodist preacher in London between 1940 and 1945, I can assure you that "Things" still go bump in the night in an ever more frightening crescendo.[2]

A third way of reading Paul's summary is even more reflective. In this way the statement is an affirmation that God's love in Christ is not defeated by anything, particularly the various forces that are observable in human history.[3] When one turns to other, similar passages (see note 1), a central concept and word appears. That central word is "power," or "powers"; other words are directly related to or interchangeable with this term.[4] "Power" is more than a word: it is a concept concerning the reality of life and the dimensions of human lostness.

The people of the New Testament, like us, lived in a power-conscious world. For them power was located in the circumstances and situations of human life. Ephesians, for instance, speaks of the "prince of the power of the air" (2:2). This phrase has behind it a specific view of the heavens, the earth, and the air that was current at that time. Nevertheless, the phrase "of the air" is an equivalent of our modern phrase about something being "in the air"—without, of course, the cosmological trappings.[5] Things that we say are "in the air" are very powerful. The spirit of the modern age, for example, was for a long time the prince among the things that were "in the air."

Powers, in their New Testament sense, are also located in the institutions of history, as one perceives when reading about the state in the Revelation to John and when viewing both past and present events. However, "rulers of this age" (1 Cor. 2:8) and "world rulers" (Eph. 6:12) do not refer to Caesar or to specific heads of state. These terms refer to the powers, or forces, of world history. Thus the rulers of this age are not our successive presidents and their counterparts in other nations but the forces of world hunger, nuclear deterrence, balance of powers, population increase, national interest, oppression, and the like.

The powers thus inhere in the multitude of circumstances that compose human affairs. They appear in the dominating spirit or idea behind any historical era. They are at the base of the institutions and forces of any and all eras of history. Scriptural language concerning the powers is neither precise nor exhaustive. Indeed, the biblical language is elusive. Yet, at the same time, the language is serious, as demonstrated by the connection it makes between the powers and Jesus through the account of the crucifixion.

Modern terms that are equivalent to "powers" may be "power structures" or, perhaps, "structures of earthly existence" or "social forces."[6]

Powers and power structures are not independent; they exist within and among peoples and peoplehood and are a part of both. There is no evidence to think that the powers are "beings" floating around, alighting now here, now there, to influence human affairs. Powers are not independent of peoples and peoplehood. On the contrary, peoples seem to have a priority over powers in the scheme of things. Primeval history does not have a separate reference that is for powers what the Table of Nations is for peoples. Indeed, the description of creative activity in the table may imply the structures of power and ordering which make such work possible in society, thus suggesting a coupling of peoplehood and powers from time immemorial. Yet God does not make a covenant with the powers; God makes a covenant with a people. The gospel has relevance to the powers, but it is preached to the peoples. The church is not constituted by people who come out of the powers, but by those who are called from the peoples of the world to be the people of God.

This priority has high importance. It suggests that while the powers cannot be escaped, an intimate relationship exists between peoplehood and the powers that operate within the peoplehood. It also suggests that while the powers are a given, inescapable part of life, they are set within peoples and exert influence because of their setting. The powers are not merely impersonal forces. Scripture frequently personifies the powers, as when calling them the "world rulers," a trait which may have derived from the close connection that exists between peoples and the powers. Imbued with the qualities of peoplehood, the powers do seem almost human. Thus, the Roman state was not only shaped by the Roman peoplehood; it also shaped that peoplehood.

The powers bear heavily upon the identity of a people, its creativity and character, but yet they do not have the final voice over them. Peoplehood is the most fundamental structure of humanity because it is what enables human life to exist. Powers are the next fundamental structure; they intertwine with peoplehood, existing in all peoples everywhere. Thus, the people of Israel shaped its structure of power, its state, law, and temple, for example. And thus America's people shapes its power structures, among them its government, economic institutions, and civil religion. The powers, in their turn, influence the peoplehood and the people. The powers provide the people with a particular shape and structure; they perform a regulatory or order-giving function within the peoplehood; they are also vehicles of creativity. If Scripture does not give the powers a place at the beginning of things, it does give them a place of honor, one that was appointed or ordained by God for these functions among peoples.[7]

Scripture, however, is not romantic about the powers; it perceives their dark side. Scripture's interest in the powers is not sociological (although it has sociological import) but theological. Viewed in this manner, the powers function for the benefit of humanity and its peoples, but they are not an unmitigated good. They participate in the darkness of the world. They are ambiguous.

The ambiguity of the powers appears nowhere more forcefully than in the crucifixion of Christ. There, the powers of state, religion, tradition, and zealotry combined to reject the light of Christ. For those who gave us the New Testament, that was the ultimate rebellion: these powers arrogated to themselves the right to put Jesus on the cross and did it. From the viewpoint of the first Christians (and later ones as well), there could be no clearer example of creature in the place of Creator. Speaking of the secret and hidden wisdom of God, now made clear, Paul writes: "None of the rulers of this age understood this; for if they had, they would not have crucified the Lord of glory" (1 Cor. 2:8).

That insight suggests a further sinister aspect of the powers. They have a certain magnetic force: they exert a pull which is always in the direction of demanding undue loyalty. The state, the law, and the various institutions of society exert this pull as do the ideas and the spirit of the times. From the time the people of Israel entered Canaan, and even during their wandering in the wilderness, Scripture records the people's struggle with religion, institutions, and the state—a struggle which invariably centers upon each power's ability to attract loyalty to itself. The exercise of this pull is never crude; it is always subtle, like the serpent's ability to tempt. The powers extend an invitation to participate in power, surely one of the most attractive invitations known to humanity. King David, using his influence to secure Bathsheba, must have certainly felt the attractiveness of power, and Judas must have also felt the attraction when the powerful messengers came to him. Both David and Judas, however, in accepting the invitation of power, soon came to realize that they were dominated by the power they had accepted. Power presents itself in the guise of empowerment, only to turn into domination.

Even though the powers of the world have a constructive function, they are also subject to the great compulsion: they themselves worship the creature and they have a magnetic attraction which plays upon the individual's compulsion to do the same. Through these routes the powers also affect the people and the peoplehood. If the constructive aspect of the powers is to give substance to the identity of the people, and thus to its creativity and character, their sinister aspect is always at hand. Even when the ideas, the institutions, the processes, and the situations of human life appear to be most glorious in achievement and in promise of achievement, they each possess the compulsion to worship the creature, played out on the grand scale. These powers of history not only can be but have been, again and again, both the cause and focus of the ultimate rebellion. In the crucifixion, and in every other form of tyranny and cruelty, they substitute themselves for God.

> For we are not contending against flesh and blood, but against the principalities, against the powers, against the world rulers of this present darkness, against the spiritual hosts of wickedness in the heavenly places. (Eph. 6:12-13)

The powers, necessary to life but infused with darkness, are the undertow of history.

12

Creature: Dependence in the Cloak of Autonomy

A short time ago my wife and I were invited to dinner at the home of a refugee family from Vietnam. After a superbly prepared Vietnamese meal, we sat on the secondhand couch in the low-standard home in central Minnesota that had been provided for the refugees, part of the stream of shunted, homeless millions who have since the thirties become a part of the world's culture. Surrounded by the large family, my wife and I looked at their picture album. It began some thirty years ago in Saigon, with pictures of their resplendent wedding, and ended with pictures of the family stripped to nothing in the Thai refugee camp and of their arrival at the reception center in California. As the album unfolded, what impressed me was not simply that most of the family's early dreams had been denied: that happens to everyone, everywhere. I was struck instead by the way war had torn them out of their land and culture, out of every inherited, surrounding influence of nurture and promise, and by the way they had been hit and swept along by history, uprooted and exiled. Even so, I was impressed that the faces of this family, while lined with tragedy, were alive with the possibility of a new beginning.

Long ago, following the brutal devastation of their home country and of things made precious by long memory, the exiles in Babylon sang a new song:

Thus says God, the Lord,
who created the heavens and stretched them out,
who spread forth the earth and what comes from it,

who gives breath to the people upon it
and spirit to those who walk in it:
"I am the Lord, I have called you in righteousness,
I have taken you by the hand and kept you;
I have given you as a covenant to the people,
a light to the nations,
to open the eyes that are blind,
to bring out the prisoners from the dungeon,
from the prison those who sit in darkness.
I am the Lord, that is my name;
my glory I give to no other,
nor my praise to graven images.
Behold, the former things have come to pass,
and new things I now declare;
before they spring forth
I tell you of them."
Sing to the Lord a new song,
his praise from the end of the earth! (Isa. 42:5–10)

Two affirmations of this song, first sung in desperation, run deeply in the biblical tradition, further illumining the human sense of being lost. One affirmation is the idea that God takes people by the hand and keeps them in righteousness; the other is that God created the heavens, the earth, and the people. Both imply a further dimension of the condition of human beings. Not only are humans subject to the destructive, inner compulsion of sin and to domination by strong powers, humans are also creatures dependent upon a power beyond human capacities. Not in control of either life or the future of life, humans are dependent, vulnerable, lost without the Creator.

These affirmations of God's leading and creating give an urgent quality to scriptural faith. God's presence moved Israel in two directions: toward salvation and toward the recognition that the Lord who saves is the God who creates. The connection between these two aspects of Israel's knowledge of God is as remarkable as it is clear. The earliest creed (see p. 11) recalls only the Exodus from Egypt, the event in which Israel came to know God; it does not center upon or indeed even mention God as the Creator. It is likely that the experience of being led forth from captivity and of being constituted a people was primary to Israel, and that this knowledge of God led to or opened out upon a wider knowledge of God the Creator. The originating experi-

ence in Egypt either was distinctive in itself or carried in itself the
embryo of their distinctive faith. Israel knew that God heard their cry of
affliction and that the Lord chose them, giving them the identity of
"my people." Furthermore, this knowledge evidently contained a
dynamic whereby the Redeemer came to be known as the Creator.
Precisely how the Hebrew mind moved from God's redemption to
God's creation is not spelled out; however, the sequence of this movement and the certitude that results from it are inescapable.

Scripture, moreover, does not leave the reader with an anemic
association of the ideas of creation and redemption:

Rejoice in the Lord, O you righteous!
Praise befits the upright.
Praise the Lord with the lyre,
    make melody to him with the harp of ten strings!
Sing to him a new song,
    play skillfully on the strings, with loud shouts.

For the word of the Lord is upright;
    and all his work is done in faithfulness.
He loves righteousness and justice;
    the earth is full of the steadfast love of the Lord.

By the word of the Lord the heavens were made,
    and all their host by the breath of his mouth.
He gathered the waters of the sea as in a bottle;
    he put the deeps in storehouses.
Let all the earth fear the Lord,
    let all the inhabitants of the world stand in awe of him!
For he spoke, and it came to be;
    he commanded, and it stood forth. (Ps. 33:1–9)

These lines present God's creativity in the same radical form that all
Scripture presents God's salvation. Both creation and salvation are
accomplished by God's Word. Creation does not occur by a process of
spilling over from a cosmic source of life and being. Creation happens
because God speaks, as in the Genesis 1 account. Creation might have
been a very big bang, or it might have been but a whisper uttered over a
very long time. Its precise form may ultimately defy imagination. One
implication, however, stands out clearly: we are decisively created.
"He spoke, and it came to be" means that. The same is true for
salvation: humans hear God's Word and respond to it. The conse-

quence is radical; creation and salvation by the Word—one wants to
say, *only* the Word?—of God accentuates the power and absoluteness
of God as well as human dependence upon God.

> In the beginning was the Word, and the Word was with God, and
> the Word was God. He was in the beginning with God; all things were
> made through him, and without him was not anything made that was
> made. . . . And the Word became flesh and dwelt among us, full of grace
> and truth. . . . (John 1:1–3, 14)

These lines and others in the New Testament perpetuate the deep
tradition and transform it.[1] The Word which God speaks—the Word of
creation and redemption—does not change. It exists always the same,
yet it once emerged in the flesh of human life, dwelling among us. For
us the mystery of this that once happened remains in the same measure as its clarity. Christ manifests what was there in the beginning: the
power of God to create and redeem; in his own flesh, Christ restates the
degree of human dependence upon God.

In Jesus' presence and language, human dependence is absolute.
When anxiety arises concerning our creaturely needs, we hear Jesus
speak of the birds and the lilies, reminding us that we are as dependent
as they and that anxiety is futile. When we are moved to love, we hear
Jesus present the "hard case," telling us that it is easy to love people
who are good to us, but that real love embraces our enemy, just as God
provides sun and rain on both the just and the unjust. When we try to
build the kingdom of God and look for the results of our work, we
remember that "the kingdom of God is as if a man should scatter seed
upon the ground, and should sleep and rise night and day, and the seed
should sprout and grow, he knows not how" (Mark 4:26; see also
Matthew 13). If the pioneer of faith and the one who makes faith
perfect does not have the fox's hole or the bird's nest but is content
with having nowhere to lay his head, we realize indirectly how great is
human dependence on these matters. If Jesus' power was so astounding that people exclaimed "What manner of man is this that even the
winds and the seas obey him?" then we see that human power is
contingent to the point of helplessness. If we are brought up short by
the abrupt "Let the dead bury the dead," perhaps it is because we are
suddenly impressed by the utter contingency of life in the face of
death. If not a sparrow falls without the Father's knowledge, then we

are also like sparrows, dependent upon God. When Jesus died there was darkness, and the earth shook. If at the end, the sun is darkened and we are judged according to standards that are the opposite of every usual human instinct, then we live constantly in the presence of these ultimate statements of human dependence and vulnerability.[2]

Even so, we fight against this dependence. One suspects that most of us, most of the time, cover up dependence by asserting our autonomy. People are created, Scripture tells us, in the "image of God" (Gen. 1:27). This is neither a reference to the moral or spiritual capabilities of human beings, nor, in a psychological mode, to something deep down in people which needs to be refurbished or allowed to shine. The holistic concept of human beings in Scripture does not permit such a moralized or internalized view of the image of God. Rather, the phrase refers to the person as a whole. In the passage where it occurs, the stress is upon the capacity and task of humans to be the representatives of God in creation and in relation to the rest of creation. "The decisive thing about man's similarity to God, therefore," writes Gerhard von Rad, "is his function in the nonhuman world."[3] This does not yield a biblical warrant for human beings to exploit and foul the natural world. It means humans must have the same care for the natural world that God has. It bespeaks a harmony in which human beings perform a divine, or at least a divinely appointed, function.

Dissonance, however, has disrupted that created and intended harmony. In human consciousness, dependence upon God recedes in favor of human autonomy, capability, and power. Mastery of the nonhuman world takes precedence over representing God in the nonhuman world. The abilities humans were given in order to be God's representatives assume a different role. These capacities and powers seem to warrant the autonomous use and management of the natural world so far as that is humanly possible. Moreover, what is humanly possible becomes, with technology's advances, a dramatically receding horizon. From the first use of fire to the first use of the atom, the dissonance caused by the autonomous use of human capacities in the natural world has been dangerous.

The refugee may be the most striking example that history provides of the contingency of human life. The accounts of Moses and the desert wandering show how acutely the Israelites felt the impact of their experience. Those refugees might have used religion to assert their autonomy, especially when they settled in Canaan. But they did not do that, neither as arrivals in Canaan nor, centuries later, as deportees to Babylon. They went the other way; they broadened the meaning and sense of dependency. The faith they were given in Egypt amid the buffeting forces of human history led them to embrace the dependence of the creature upon the Creator.

The feeling grows, upon reading, that it is not the purpose of Scripture to frighten, crush, or condemn. There is judgment in Scripture, judgment so severe that when one feels its force one knows that wisdom truly begins with the fear of God (Prov. 9:10). Scripture speaks of the human condition in order to be helpful. When it speaks of sin, it is to provide self-understanding and to show how the power of sin's compulsion may be broken. When it speaks of the powers, it is to illumine the social environment and to provide hope in the face of what otherwise is crushing. When it speaks of the dependence of the creature, it is to make clear that everything is in the hands of God. Whenever Scripture describes these aspects of humanity's basic condition, being lost without God, one finds the graciousness of God—not vaguely, but in identifiable forms which in turn suggest a definite spirituality.

13

Lost: The Meeting Point of God and the Human Spirit

The people of Scripture, found and touched by God, knew what it meant to be without God and lost. Over time and within diverse experience, those who listened and heard, who heard and followed, and who, following, found the going difficult, learned that life proceeds under certain conditions. These conditions go beyond temporary difficulties; they are constant aspects of human life, limits encountered within the texture of human existence, boundaries beyond which human effort cannot go on its own. The fact that we humans must live as peoples and within a peoplehood is one such limit. Being lost, wandering in darkness, is another limit, one of such scope that Scripture describes in detail three of its component parts: being sinful, being subject to powers, and being creatures. By the testimony of Scripture, these limits stand between humans and God. Put the other way, the Hebraic encounter with God produced the perception, the disclosure or revelation, that God's graciousness breaks into human life at points where human life is limited.

Biblical language, blunt and vigorous, clearly states the seriousness of these limits for human relationships with God. But the matter does not end there. The people of Scripture discovered a further aspect of their own situation and of God's ways with human beings. It became clear that these limitations exert immense pressure upon human life, and that this pressure is part of God's way with humanity. As understood in Scripture, the pressure, sometimes all but unbearably acute, enables humans to know that God is in action at these boundaries. The biblical word for this pressure is "wrath."

In the early fifties, when I was a part-time minister of a black church in Queens, New York City, word came that a young woman—highly educated, unemployed, active in the congregation—had broken down. According to the report, it happened when she was standing in line at an unemployment office. Suddenly she lashed out, screaming and swinging her umbrella. There was no information as to the provocation. The result was her commitment to a huge state institution for the mentally ill. After a time I secured permission see her. At the institution I reported to a uniformed doctor and was told that she would be brought down to his office. She appeared, between two male attendants. I smiled, put out my hand, and said hello. Instantly, with angered face, she lunged at me, fingers clawing. She also screamed profanities, which culminated in two words, "white minister," hurled with the force of a snapping whip. The two attendants seized her before she could reach me, wrestled her to the floor where she fought hard as they struggled, hitting, to get her into a straitjacket. They succeeded. Standing alone in the doorway, I watched her being forcefully led down the corridor between the two attendants. Her desperate wailing and sobbing echoed within the barren walls. Turning to the doctor, a white male like the two attendants and me, I learned what I already knew: the pressure of racial oppression had stirred her anger to the breaking point.

I sat, seared and silent. I had seen horrible suffering of an innocent: my black friend was not responsible for the oppression that was destroying her. I had hoped that my ministry in the church in Queens bore some testimony, however slight, against that oppression which I did not want or cause. Yet my white face was for her the symbol of oppression, and it turned church into an aggravation, not a ministry. I was caught. I could not dissociate myself from my face. All this I knew in a flash. Later, I realized that this encounter—its symbols and our participation in them—contained more than innocence, suffering, anger, failure, sorrow, and guilt. In this episode there was something that pertained to each person present and to human history as a whole, something that characterized humanity which none of us could escape. We had been engulfed by human wrath and had felt the rumblings of the wrath of God.

At the beginning of Romans, following a few introductory lines, Paul presents a remarkable view of humanity and of God:

> For the wrath of God is revealed from heaven against all ungodliness and wickedness of men who by their wickedness suppress the truth. For what can be known about God is plain to them, because God has shown it to them. Ever since the creation of the world his invisible nature, namely, his eternal power and deity, has been clearly perceived in the things that have been made. So they are without excuse; for although they knew God they did not honor him as God or give thanks to him, but they became futile in their thinking and their senseless minds were darkened. Claiming to be wise, they became fools, and exchanged the glory of the immortal God for images resembling mortal man or birds or animals or reptiles. Therefore, God gave them up. . . . (Rom. 1:18–24a)

This almost offensively bold language speaks of the two types of wrath known by the authors of Scripture. One type is the wrath of humanity. The other is the wrath of God. They are distinct but related. The wrath of humanity is characterized by ungodliness, by wickedness which suppresses the truth, and by futility and darkness of mind. These all stem from the rebellion that exchanges the glory of God for images. Carrying the matter further, Paul employs a strange, harsh phrase, repeated three times: "therefore God gave them up." Because of rebellion against God, "God gave them up in the lusts of their hearts to impurity" (1:24); "God gave them up to dishonorable passions" (1:26); "God gave them up to a base mind and to improper conduct" (1:28). Clearly it is not a casual phrase. It confirms freedom, even the freedom to rebel against God, but that does not seem to be its main point. "God gave them up" warns that there are consequences of rebellion, and that these consequences are filled with wrath.

When I sat in the cavernous hospital listening to the angered shrieks of my black friend, the consequences of oppression—the white wickedness which for centuries had suppressed the truth about God's creatures, the base mind and improper conduct of whole populations of white people, and the complicity of Christianity in all of this—were gathered up in rage and violence. We were enmeshed in the consequences of this ugly history, and God had not prevented either the consequences or their impact upon us but had given us up to them. Yet God had not gone away. Within the human wrath there was also the wrath of God.

The people of Scripture possessed a knowledge of God that, if it first

offends, it then staggers the mind, inspiring awe. Those people came
to know and understand God's anger. The account in primeval history
of God's anger with humanity and of God's consequent action with
Noah and the flood, together with the events of the wilderness journey
under Moses, register a theme of Scripture: when God is denied by
human wickedness, God reacts with anger. People can turn away from
God and God's love, but they cannot be finished with God. The people
of Scripture knew that God's anger is not whimsical, arbitrary, and
unrelated to neglect or denial of God. In their experience, God's graciousness included both anger and love. Feeling the force of God's
anger, they knew that the wrath of God resulted from wounded love. [1]

The anger of God's wounded love is a special kind of anger, as is clear
in the Exodus story. There plagues and slaughter from God figure in
almost superabundant measure. One might read of these events mechanically, in the sense that since the Egyptians would not let Israel
go, they were punished. Yet the tenor of the accounts does not permit
such an easy reading. They convey outrage at the oppression and
anger that affliction which caused the people to cry to heaven would
continue. But one also senses that even though God's love was
wounded, it still continues.

Isaiah describes the anger of wounded love more sharply. Two
passages reflect the prophet's early hope and later experience:

> The people who walked in darkness
>   have seen a great light;
> those who dwelt in a land of deep darkness,
>   on them has light shined. . . .
> For to us a child is born,
>   to us a son is given. . . .
> The Lord has sent a word against Jacob,
>   and it will light upon Israel. . . .
> Therefore the Lord does not rejoice over their young men,
>   and has no compassion on their fatherless and widows;
> for everyone is godless and an evildoer,
>   and every mouth speaks folly.
> For all this his anger is not turned away
>   and his hand is stretched out still. (Isa. 9:2, 6, 8, 17)

With Isaiah one feels the tenderness and hope of God and, at the
same time, the hard face of "darkness" and of "no compassion."

Neither God nor God's anger goes away. The hand remains out-
stretched.

What makes God angry? Isaiah gives the answer: "The people did
not turn to him who smote them, nor seek the Lord of Hosts" (Isa.
9:13). That is, in fact, the constant answer of all of Scripture. When
people turn away and worship something else, God's love is hurt and
God's anger gathers. Three instances further illumine the matter: the
misuse of virtue, cruelty among people, and the refusal of God's
invitation.

The haunting, dramatic poem of Job tells of God's anger at the
misuse of human virtue. In spite of the terrible troubles visited upon
him, Job continued to press the claims of his own virtue. In Job's view,
virtue was an entitlement program, guaranteeing just treatment at the
hands of the Almighty. Job could not see the point of God's argument:

> Then the Lord answered Job out of the whirlwind:
> "Gird up your loins like a man;
>   I will question you, and you declare to me.
> Will you even put me in the wrong?
> Will you condemn me that you may be justified?" (Job 40:6–8)

"This question," writes Samuel Terrien, "penetrated to the heart of the
debate. . . . Job did not come to this moment in a spiritual vacuum.
With the proud conscience of moral man, he had demanded an audi-
ence. He now discovered sinfulness not as moral transgression but as
the pride of self-deification."[2]

Job's assumptions and his experience of God's condemnation—
"therefore I despise myself, and repent in dust and ashes" (Job
42:6)—are not isolated. They lend, for example, sharp clarity to Jesus'
anger in the synagogue. He wished to heal a man on the Sabbath, but
was surrounded by those who disapproved.

> And he said to them, "Is it lawful on the sabbath to do good or to do harm,
> to save life or to kill?" But they were silent. And he looked around at them
> with anger, grieved at their hardness of heart, and said to the man,
> "Stretch out your hand." He stretched it out, and his hand was restored.
> (Mark 3:4–5)

The poetry of Job and the drama in the synagogue run parallel. Virtue
may be personally inherited as it was with Job, or it may be embodied in
laws and institutions as it was with those in the synagogue. When,

however, virtue elevates the self to the point where God cannot be heard, it ceases to be virtue and becomes a mask, evoking wrath.

Cruelty also evokes God's wrath, as is seen by the Word from God spoken by the prophet Amos:

> "Hear this word, you cows of Bashan,
> who are in the mountain of Samaria,
> who oppress the poor, who crush the needy,
>   who say to their husbands, 'Bring, that we may drink!'
> The Lord God has sworn by his holiness
>   that, behold, the days are coming upon you,
> when they shall take you away with hooks,
>   even the last of you with fishhooks." (Amos 4:1–2)

The self-serving cruelty addressed by Amos has other forms which are also universal to human experience. In Jesus' parable the king vented his wrath upon the servant:

> "Then his lord summoned him and said to him, 'You wicked servant! I forgave you all that debt because you besought me; and should not you have had mercy on your fellow servant, as I had mercy on you?' And in anger his lord delivered him to the jailers, till he should pay all his debt. So also my heavenly Father will do to every one of you, if you do not forgive your brother from your heart." (Matt. 18:32–35)

The language of Amos conveys God's anger indirectly; Jesus' parable is direct. Moreover, besides describing God's anger, it also describes the kingdom of God. In Jesus' words (see also Matt. 25:31–46), one discerns a movement between God's anger and human cruelty that simultaneously goes in two directions. Specific actions in this life are seen in relation to the last, ultimate time of human existence with God, and the final reality of God's kingdom is shown to have immediate bearing upon the present moment of life. To state it succinctly, God's combination of love and anger simultaneously moves toward life's present moment as well as its ultimate moment. In this framework, when everything is a "now" and nothing can be put off, God's wrath is a warning. God speaks in anger now against present cruelty; cruelty inflicted now has a bearing upon the ultimate moment when the kingdom of God finally comes. The same is true for other aspects of life and for God's relation to them.

Another parable of Jesus illustrates a third way that God's wrath is evoked. In the parable we see that divine wrath stirs over human

refusal to accept the invitation of God. When the servant reported that
those invited had refused to come to the great banquet:

> ". . . the householder in anger said to his servant, 'Go out quickly to the
> streets and lanes of the city, and bring in the poor and maimed and blind
> and lame.' And the servant said, 'Sir, what you commanded has been
> done, and still there is room.' And the master said to the servant, 'Go out to
> the highways and hedges, and compel people to come in, that my house
> may be filled. For I tell you, none of those men who were invited shall taste
> my banquet.' " (Luke 14:21–24)

Many meanings lie in this parable, but the anger in God's love
overarches them all. Neither this parable nor any scriptural experience of God's wrath generally permits a clear, dogmatic conclusion as
to the precise meaning and consequences of wrath. Will the moment
come when the householder's invitation will be withdrawn, when
those who refused to attend will never again be asked to taste the
banquet? I cannot find a clear-cut, hard line in Scripture at this point.
Yet I find testimony to the wrath of God. Whether God's love is
wounded by overblown virtue, cruelty, the refusal to accept God's
invitation, or other actions,[3] two affirmations seem clear in Scripture:
(1) rebellion against God produces a life filled with wrath; (2) when the
neglect and disdain that accompany rebellion turn God's love away,
God not only can but does respond with wrath. Both the wrath of
humanity and the wrath of God are real. These affirmations, however,
lead to a further question.

What is the function of human wrath and God's wrath? To appreciate the answer we need to backtrack a little. Scripture unmistak-
ably distinguishes between human wrath and the wrath of God, but it
also insists upon a close connection between them. This connection is
complex because divine wrath is never pure anger, but a combination
of anger and love. Human rebellion against God, and the wrathful
troubles it entails, are always met by anger encompassed by love. The
most severe warnings of the prophets to Israel—"I have consumed
them with the fire of my wrath" (Ezek. 22:31)—breathe the possibility
of restoration; the demonstration of God's wrath is enveloped in patience (Rom. 9:22–24); the final, universal warning to all people is set
within the special wrath of Christ's sacrifice (Rev. 6:15–17). If human
and divine wrath are always distinguished from each other, they are

also melded, so that human wrath is interpreted in the light of God's wrath, and the whole is interpreted in the light of God's purpose.

Taken in this sense, the function of wrath becomes clear. Its function is not, one should note, mere or arbitrary punishment. If I was punished, as indeed I was, in the encounter with the young black woman in the mental institution, it was not punishment for punishment's sake. Wrath has a different, twofold function, a function related to God's purpose.

First, wrath demonstrates, as perhaps only it can, that the limits of human life are not only boundaries but are also severe, serious pressure points upon life and upon human relationships to God. Wrath functions to warn us that the needle on the boiler hovers at the top. Wrath stands on the borderline between life and death, light and darkness.[4]

Most of us do not experience wrath of scriptural intensity. Or do we? Do we not know something of wrath within the soul, however secret or acknowledged? When surveying societies both past and present, does anyone feel unaware of wrath? Perhaps. Some say that internal or public difficulties are evidence that humanity has not progressed far enough, or that management skills are not well developed, or that we are only beginning to learn how to modify behavior, and that we shall advance on all fronts in due course. At one level much of this is true. But at a deeper level of life is it not also true that there is a wrath that wells up within person and society, and stalks, threatens, and seizes us all, irrespective of skills, power, and status? Is it not also true that this wrath dispels any idea that the limits of our life are only artificial or hypothetical? The compulsion we know as sin, the powers that affect us and our societies, the dependence of which we are fearful and against which we assert a supposed autonomy—these forms of our lost state are not only boundaries, confining life. They are also limits that contain power. Each possesses a reflexive power that backlashes. Sin is self-worship, and self-exaltation backlashes, causing damage to the self. The powers backlash by enticing and then corrupting not only the individual but whole peoples and civilizations. Creation backlashes when we damage the world of the human creature and the world of nature. These worlds then present complex threats to life. Another word for this backlash is "wrath," the wrathful state of humanity, enmeshed in rebellion and wickedness, to which the anger of God's wounded love sometimes gives us over.

Let us shift the language. Today in the United States we speak more and more of troubles: a troubled mind, a troubled economy, society, people, world scene. Scripture enables us to recognize the significance of these troubles. It has us perceive in them the rumblings of wrath and, on occasion, its full force. In this sense wrath is an interpretation of the troubles of self and society which we observe and feel. Wrath is not a flame thrower in the hand of divinity. Wrath emerges in the course of life, a warning.

That is the first function of wrath. The second is to show where graciousness takes hold. In an overall sense, one byproduct of all that Scripture tells us about peoples and about the components of our lost condition is that it shows there is both a wrong and a right way of turning to God. We turn to God in the wrong way when we ask for help in things that matter or seem to matter to us but which are not crucial to our relation to God. We go in the right direction, however, when we turn to God in pivotal matters: our peoplehood and personal appropriation of it, and our own manifestation of the elements of human lostness. At these points wrath gathers, accumulates, and functions positively. It shows us how and where we have wounded God, and where a turn to God meets the graciousness of God. Wrath is a signpost. We do not have to thrash around in social turmoil and personal agony; we can turn with the assurance of getting somewhere. "The wrath of God is the onslaught of the holy God asserting and establishing his absolute claim to dominion."[5]

The wrath of God is enveloped in divine patience. "Or do you presume upon the riches of his kindness and forbearance and patience?" asks Paul, writing of wrath and judgment (Rom. 2:4). The onslaught of God is wrath delayed—delayed by the graciousness of God, which is met precisely at these limits; by the graciousness of wounded love, in which anger and love are gathered together; by the graciousness which, in Krister Stendahl's phrase, holds "one inch more of mercy."[6] "The wrath," writes Abraham Heschel, "is not the end, nor is suffering an absolute. The experience is dark, to be sure, but in the darkness caused by God, there is God and there is light."[7]

14

Crossing the Boundary:
Deep Calls to Deep

We approach the heart of spirituality from the perspective that humanity is lost without God. A summary is now in order.

In their historic, intense encounter with God, the people of Scripture gained knowledge of themselves. Their experience stripped away the nonessentials. They saw that human beings are limited and that the limitations appear in constant forms. These limits are not accidental; they do not result from ignorance or primitivism. They are built-in. One limitation is that humans must live as a people, bonded together by some particular sense of peoplehood. Another limitation is that humans are captives: to sin and a false sense of freedom, to domination by powers and a false sense of power, and to dependence which results in a false sense of autonomy. The experience of these limiting conditions is variously expressed: as death in contrast to life, as darkness in contrast to light, and as being lost in contrast to being at home.

Two themes accompany these fundamentals of the human condition:

Peoples and peoplehood and the elements of our lost state mutually affect one another. Both peoples and peoplehood sin, they are subject to the powers, and they pride themselves on their autonomy—each in their own particular ways.

God is neither unconcerned nor cruel but gracious toward humanity. God creates and provides for persons and peoples and requires commitment and trust. God desires human response, and persons and peoples are capable of response to God. Wrath

ensues when human limitations are allowed to corrupt, turn
aside, or deny the graciousness and love of God.

Today we are faced with vast troubles of both person and society.
The modern mentality inclines to seek solutions in specialized realms
of knowledge. Psychic aspects of what Scripture calls sin evoke from
moderns a psychological/educational—in any case a developmen-
tal—solution. When present-day powers threaten, moderns are quick
to advocate an interdisciplinary array of specialists, those skilled in
everything from politics to the arts. When either nature or neighbor
threatens our autonomy, contemporary attention turns to virtually the
whole range of sciences, from physics to embryology, in order to
reestablish autonomy at a less precarious level. A specialized culture
and society brings its specialized knowledge to bear upon its fundamental problems.

As it should. The "should" is strongly warranted by Scripture's
encouragement of creativity, but this encouragement itself brings
forth a warning. Peril lurks in placing too much confidence in the
capacity of human creativity to solve problems that stem from inherent
human limitations. Moreover, Scripture has interests beyond the encouragement of cultural or social creativity. Scripture has its eye not
only upon the activities of the individual, society, and culture, but also
upon the relation of these to the ultimate state of human beings before
God. Scripture goes beyond human achievement and crises which,
however glorious or portentous, signify limits to human life and confine human effort to darkness. Freedom and life lie beyond, to be
achieved not by the disciplines of human knowledge but by the action
of God.[1]

As a hart longs
for flowing streams
so longs my soul
    for thee, O God.
My soul thirsts for God,
    for the living God.
When shall I come and behold
    the face of God? . . .

My soul is cast down within me,
    therefore I remember thee
from the land of Jordan and of Hermon,

from Mount Mizar.
Deep calls to deep
  at the thunder of thy cataracts;
all thy waves and thy billows
  have gone over me.
By day the Lord commands his steadfast love;
  and at night his song is with me,
  a prayer to the God of my life.

I say to God, my rock;
  "Why has thou forgotten me?
Why go I mourning
  because of the oppression of the enemy?"
As with a deadly wound in my body,
  my adversaries taunt me,
while they say to me continually,
  "Where is your God?"

Why are you cast down, O my soul,
  and why are you disquieted within me? (Ps. 42:1, 2, 6–11a)

When the soul is cast down, not by passing moods but by the pressures of life, when wrath rumbles—deep calls to deep. Then boundaries are crossed, action takes place, and the psalm is finished.

Hope in God; for I shall again praise him,
  my help and my God.[2] (Ps. 42:11b)

The Bible is a book of focus: God's graciousness, God's action with humanity, is focused in Jesus Christ. Focused. Anyone who only dabbles in photography knows the importance of being in focus. A person who suffers from a cataract sees only a blurred diffusion of light until, after an operation, the correct lens is put in place. Then shape and color, depth and perspective suddenly appear. So the graciousness of God springs forth in Christ. His advent, presence, and departure almost immediately produced astonishing claims as to the meaning of his life. These claims stretched to the cosmic, ultimate, and trans-historical reaches of imagination and penetrated as well to the histori-cal, immediate, and intimate realms of life. Of this One it was said, in language of wonderful variety, that he restored light, made captives free, presented life anew, and opened the future. This language gives true shape and color, depth and perspective to the relation between God and humanity.

The graciousness of God, focused in Jesus Christ, has a definite form, which is described in the following three passages.

Behold, my servant shall prosper,
  he shall be exalted and lifted up . . .

He was despised and rejected by men;
  a man of sorrows, and acquainted with grief . . .

Surely he has borne our griefs
  and carried our sorrows . . .
upon him was the chastisement that made us whole . . .

like a lamb that is led to the slaughter . . .
  so he opened not his mouth.
By oppression and judgment he was taken away . . .

the will of the Lord shall prosper in his hand. . . .
by his knowledge shall the righteous one, my servant,
  make many to be accounted righteous . . .
because he poured out his soul to death. (Isa. 52:13—53:12)

In the beginning was the Word, and the Word was with God, and the Word was God. . . . In him was life, and the life was the light of men. . . . He came to his own home, and his own people received him not. . . . And the Word became flesh and dwelt among us, full of grace and truth; we have beheld his glory, glory as of the only Son from the Father. . . . No one has ever seen God; the only Son, who is in the bosom of the Father, he was made him known. (John 1:1-18)

Christ Jesus, who, though he was in the form of God, did not count equality with God a thing to be grasped, but emptied himself, taking the form of a servant. . . . he humbled himself and became obedient unto death, even death on a cross. Therefore God has highly exalted him . . . (Phil. 2:5-11)

The passage from Isaiah and others similar to it (Isa. 42:1-9; 49:1-13; 50:4-9) are unique in the scriptural writing that precedes Christ. Profound, enigmatic, the songs of the servant, conceived in the period of exile, have no parallel. They clearly stand within Israel's tradition of the chosen people, yet they perceive the meaning of "chosen" with a unique depth. From earliest times Christians have seen in these lines from Isaiah a description of Jesus so powerful and accurate that they have regarded him as their fulfillment.

The passages from John's Gospel and Paul's letter to the Philippians are hymns that were used in the worship of the earliest Christian communities. They come not from "theological minds" but from the inwardness of early devotion to Christ. These and other hymns used in the New Testament writings show us what the first Christians shared with one another about Jesus and what they shared with God about the One who had come among them.

These passages illuminate the form of God's graciousness. Directly or indirectly, they state that the graciousness of God appears in the human form of a servant, and they describe the form of the servant in a certain way.[3] In almost crude phrases—"no form or comeliness," "no beauty," "the world knew him not," "even death on a cross"—these passages direct attention away from any possible attractiveness of shape. In these passages attention is instead concentrated upon motion.

The motion is rhythmic. It does not proceed from one place to another but from one quality to another. It begins with the will of the unnamed One. It moves from the life that is light, from the form of God and of being with God, and proceeds to the realm of darkness, suffering, rejection, and death. This self-emptying motion of the Servant, this light coming into the world, has purpose. The purpose is not to supplant, conquer, or subdue. It is to absorb, to take the iniquities of us all into himself, to give grace upon grace, to give power to those who will receive it, to make God known, and to make many to be counted as righteous. This self-emptying movement of the Servant has a power which startles the nations; the will of the Lord prospers in his hand. The grace and truth of God within this Man of Sorrows lead to a "therefore": therefore every knee "shall bow and every tongue confess that Jesus Christ is Lord" (Phil. 2:11). This apparent weakness, expressed in this Servant who before the final hour washes the feet of his followers and at the final hour of life is álone, contains a power that goes beyond the cosmic boundaries to the very glory of God. Thus the Servant embodies the rhythm of divine grace, and the rhythm of divine grace is embodied in the Servant. In him God moves into the pain and rejection of the world and, from the silence of his suffering "for all," brings forth victory.

These passages are not isolated. They lead into other descriptions and expressions of Christ and his meaning. Think of the various titles given to Christ that are found in the New Testament.[4] "Servant of the Lord" is one title, but there are many others: Prophet, High Priest, Messiah, Son of Man, Lord, Savior, Word, Son of God. Yet, in a sometimes unspoken, sometimes explicit way, the servant theme runs throughout all the titles. The title "Word" is conferred, for instance, upon Jesus in the passage from John reproduced above, but the passage embodies essential characteristics of the servant rhythm,[5] and this is understood to originate in the "bosom of the Father." If we think of Hebrews and the high priest who mediates God to us, that high priest is no esoteric, merely cultic figure, but one who "learned obedience through what he suffered" (Heb. 5:8). Thus, Christ forever revolutionizes the cult and its worship. Similarly, the recognition that Jesus performs the priestly act of leading us to God prevents any tendency to reduce the Servant of God to terms that connote (although they always include) humanitarian service only. If we think of the Messiah, that figure who is to come is the Servant upon whom has been laid the iniquity of us all, and the humbled Servant is the One who stands at the end of time.

Scripture therefore presents us with a focus, but it does not permit that focus to be mechanically managed. Neither one angle nor one distance suffices. The books of the New Testament differ so sharply from each other as to tempt some to see little unity among them, and, from some narrow focus of a literary or historical nature, the unity is difficult to discern.[6] The difficulty, however, results from myopia. The variety in the New Testament contains a unity, if one refuses to be mechanical or nearsighted when searching for it. Indeed, one scarcely needs to search. The various New Testament authors testified that they knew, because of either immediate or more distant experience, the person in whom the graciousness of God was manifest. "We have beheld his glory" is a universal affirmation of these books. That is their unity: they speak, in varied accents and from varied perspectives, of the One who lived at the boundaries and by whose life the boundaries were crossed.

Within all the varieties of New Testament perspective, however, there is a central, rhythmic action. The New Testament does not merely depict a figure; it speaks primarily of the action of that figure.

> For I delivered to you as of first importance what I also received, that
> Christ died for our sins in accordance with the scriptures, that he was

buried, that he was raised on the third day in accordance with the scriptures, and that he appeared to Cephas, then to the twelve. (1 Cor. 15:3–5)

This fundamental tradition of Paul and the earliest Christians concentrates upon the action of crucifixion and resurrection.[7] If the New Testament books are united by the person of Christ which they variously portray, the crux of this person's life is his crucifixion and resurrection. This action, done for all, embraces the supreme servant act, the act which astonishes and defies comprehension, the act to which all the other actions of Jesus relate and from which they all draw their meaning. *This action exhibits the unexpected rhythm of rejection and acceptance, of defeat and victory by which the Servant of God transforms all servitude. It is this act which changes the servilities of our lost condition into the transcendent power of those who follow and obey.* The title "Lord" formed the substance of what may be the earliest of creeds: "Jesus Christ is Lord." If so one may imagine that it was no murmured repetition of dogma but an exultant shout, for it signified that the Lord was not another triumphalist ruler but the self-emptying One whose life, ended by crucifixion, was resurrected.

If one allows it to do so, this sequence of crucifixion-resurrection-Lord retrieves and tells the whole story of the good news. The title "Lord" sprang joyously from those first worshiping lips because of the experience that told them that Jesus was alive.[8] The way in which Mark began his Gospel indicates what was at stake in that experience:

Now after John was arrested, Jesus came into Galilee, preaching the gospel of God, and saying, "The time is fulfilled, and the kingdom of God is at hand: repent, and believe in the gospel." (Mark 1:14–15)

Either Jesus had gone down under the weight of crucifixion and death and the gospel of God was not true, or the crucifixion, utterly real even to Jesus' forsaken cry, was not final, Jesus lived, and the gospel of God was true. To exclaim "Lord" was to acknowledge that God had vindicated Jesus' life and death by a resurrection of that life.[9] What, however, does vindication mean?

The answer lies in the fact that no New Testament writer gives any warrant for doing violence to the sequence of crucifixion-resurrection-Lord, a violence which either would make the crucifixion a formal prelude to the resurrection or would cut the resurrection out. Such

violence, of course, takes different forms. Whenever the church, em-
phasizing Christ's victory, exercise power over others, it violates the
character of the victory which has been won because of the crucifixion. Similarly, the obedience of the cross and the victory of the
resurrection are violated when Christians, in either private wishes or
public proclamations, make the gospel or faith in God the instrument
for humans to use to achieve peace of mind, prosperity, and other
desirable but inevitably self-serving ends. In a classic description,
Richard Niebuhr stated the extent to which such instrumental views
pervert the gospel: "A God without wrath brought men without sin into
a kingdom without judgment through the ministrations of a Christ
without a cross."[10]

Every New Testament writer insists upon the inherent integrity of
the crucial sequence of crucifixion-resurrection-Lord, for in it the
strange nature of God's power becomes clear. Jesus described God's
power when he said that the kingdom of God is like a mustard seed
(Matt. 13:31-32; Mark 4:30-32; Luke 13:18-19), and he exhibited it
even though it was not recognized when he hung stripped and forsaken on the cross. Except for the resurrection, the Creator's power
would not have been seen there or in the mustard seed. But the
character of the resurrection's power would not have been discerned
without the death on the cross. This tight, no indissoluble sequence
holds a vindicating finality within itself which both permitted the
triumph of "Lord" and defined henceforth the character of all final
triumph. In the person of Christ, deep calls to deep.

15

The Always-New World
of Spirituality
in Christ

The utter mystery and the intense clarity of God that are united in the figure of Christ offer a new world in which to live. This is not merely a new world for the religious life, as if God-in-Christ offers a better religion, a higher degree of cult and worship than other religions offer. The new world of Christ embraces life itself. In Christ, God offers the way out of captivity—release from the endemic confines within which life may move here and there but never beyond. God-in-Christ provides entrance to the realm of God, not simply in the sense of the future, but in the sense of a present which has a future. This realm has various descriptions. It is the kingdom of God; it is eternal life; it is life in the Spirit; it is being in Christ; it is participation in the plan of God.

The varied names and phrases go beyond the powers of human definition and yet introduce mind and heart to a realm beyond the boundaries. If at one moment the requirements of love or of the teachings of Jesus strike us with force, honesty acknowledges that although we cannot live up to either, they nevertheless carry us beyond simple imitation. If Christ is extolled as the hope of enlightened civilization, scriptural language about Christ tells us that he is also the judge of all civilizations, and that even the most brilliant human cultural achievement does not approximate the kingdom into which he leads us. If, placing high premium upon comfort, we perceive that Jesus offers the comfort of God, we are not thereby entitled to claim that Jesus merely serves our comfort, but we are enabled to see that the comfort that is in Christ transcends what we understand by that term. When, by virtue of lifelong or recent experience, our church has become so important that we think of Jesus primarily as the founder and head of the church, biblical testimony leads us beyond that to recognize the Christ who unveils God's plan not only for the church but for all of human history and all of time. Scripture constantly corrects our domesticated appreciations of Christ, presenting him afresh as the One who makes it possible for humans to be reconciled with God and to live within and yet beyond the confines inherent in our humanity.

This impact of Christ upon human life is an integral part of the reality conveyed by the New Testament writers. Their presentation of Christ, varied and yet unified, does not rest content with merely telling the story of Jesus. They describe Jesus' impact upon them, their life as a consequence of his impact, and the tradition about Jesus that stemmed from their experience of him. Put another way, these New Testament Christians were involved with Jesus. They were involved with him not only because some of them had known him and wished to follow him, but because the presence of God-in-Christ continued with them in an unmistakable way.

They found themselves caught up in a unique repetition of what, in Jesus' life, had been done for all. This repetition was different from an attempt to imitate Jesus, although there was a sufficient tendency toward imitation to inaugurate a respected subtradition in the history of his followers. Nor did the repetition of Jesus' life consist mainly in following Jesus' commandments as a new law or as a new teaching, although these too became elements in the tradition. *Rather, the repetition consisted of an inner reenactment of the crucifixion and resurrection, understood as an inner dying and being reborn.* This reenactment, so powerful as to bring about a shift in personal identity (see chapter 8), was understood to be the result of accepting and participating in the rhythmic, servant act of Christ, done for all. This did not come about by the believers' own efforts, but by the graciousness of God which had been apparent in Jesus. In this experience of dying and rebirth they were enabled and empowered by a Spirit, the Spirit of God, the Spirit which they knew to be holy, the Spirit which they spoke of as belonging both to God and to Christ. This Spirit supplied the connecting power, the enabling continuity between them and Christ. This experience and knowledge runs deep in the New Testament.[1] Here it is described by Paul:

> If the Spirit of him who raised Jesus from the dead dwells in you, he who raised Christ Jesus from the dead will give life to your mortal bodies also through his Spirit which dwells in you. (Rom. 8:11)

What makes it possible for this mortal body to have what Paul calls "life"? If the Spirit supplies the enabling continuity between me and Christ, what makes it possible for this Spirit to dwell in me? To these questions the New Testament has a clear-cut answer: faith. But at the center of that word there is a necessary, risky component: trust. When faith is mentioned, it is natural to think first of belief. "I have faith" means "I believe." Moreover, faith carries with it the idea of commitment; one has faith in, and believes in, something or someone. Trust, however, is the third element that gives faith its edge. "I believe in this and I trust it" is different from simply "I believe in this." "I am committed to this and I trust it" adds a sharp test to the commitment. Is it worth one's trust? What I really trust, do not hedge, feel no need to be cautious about, give myself to and thus make myself vulnerable to— that is what I have faith in.

We noted on p. 59 that trust, in the context of the phrase "faith/trust," is the decisive element in the formation of a new identity within the people of God. Trust is also decisive when people, wandering lost amid the varied fortunes of life, look for a true homeland. What, amid all the guesses and promises, can be trusted? From their own experience the people of the New Testament reply: God can be trusted, and Christ can be trusted to lead human beings to God.

Trust is no vague virtue, valuable in itself. New Testament Christians ask us to trust the particular love made evident by the Servant of God. This self-emptying and loving content of God's graciousness goes far, embracing the thirsty and hungry, the sick and outcast, prisoners, the homeless, those close and those who are enemies, those who follow Jesus and all the rest of the world. The love associated with the form of the Servant of God also goes deep:

> Love is patient and kind; love is not jealous or boastful; it is not arrogant or rude. Love does not insist on its own way; it is not irritable or resentful; it does not rejoice at wrong, but rejoices in the right. Love bears all things, believes all things, hopes all things, endures all things. (1 Cor. 13:4–7)

This love, which goes far and deep, is never a general sentiment, but always specific:

And he said to him, "You shall love the Lord your God with all your heart, and with all your soul, and with all your mind. This is the great and first commandment. And a second is like it, You shall love your neighbor as yourself. On these two commandments depend all the law and the prophets." (Matt. 22:37–40)

Trust in this love transforms sin—the compulsive, limiting worship of the creature. It is obvious that servant love, the love of God-in-Christ for humanity, stands in opposition to human self-love. Sin aggrandizes the self; the Servant empties the self. Sin obeys the creature; the Servant obeys God. Sin is for the self; the Servant is for all. This is all clear, but what is not so obvious is how a person can get from the one to the other. How can the crushing limit that human self-love imposes upon life be broken? By trust, the New Testament replies. The first Christians invited a specific trust in the Servant of God.

What is the result? What may one expect if one opens oneself, if one asks and it is given? Clearly, one does not cease to sin. "I believe, help my unbelief" (Mark 9:24) is a confession which conveys its own comfort and hope, as does the acute self-awareness of the apostle: "I can will what is right, but I cannot do it" (Rom. 7:18). But one can have an experience beyond sin, an experience in which knowledge dawns that sin is not all there is, that captivity to its compulsion is not forever. An experience like this is conclusive. It amounts to a genuine foretaste, an awareness that a plan is being worked out, that something is coming, not in the sense of progress plodding toward it, but in the sense that it will break through and be established. It is like a partly cloudy sky: the brilliance breaks through here and there, giving promise that it will overcome the clouds and the clear sky will prevail. If clouds close in, rains blow, and night comes dark and cold, the vision of the sun through the clouds will remain with those who viewed it, giving hope and assurance.

One may further expect that this life beyond sin is found and nourished within a people (see pp. 61–62). The quality of life in God's realm carries with it an element of the lonely journey, as Jesus' life—from his temptation to the cross—demonstrates, but it is not solitary in the individualistic meaning of the term. Even the solitude required by life in the kingdom of God is set within a community.

In chapter 8 we noted that the community of believers offers a new identity in Christ. A few paragraphs ago we spoke of the New Testament conviction that in this people the life of Christ continues, a reenactment empowered by the Spirit of God which was in Christ. For this the New Testament has dramatic language:

> "I do not pray for these only, but also for those who are to believe in me through their word, that they may all be one; even as thou, Father, art in me, and I in thee, that they also may be in us, so that the world may believe that thou hast sent me. The glory which thou hast given me I have given to them, that they may be one even as we are one, I in them and thou in me, that they may become perfectly one, so that the world may know that thou hast sent me and hast loved them even as thou has loved me." (John 17:20-23)

> For just as the body is one and has many members, and all the members of the body, though many, are one body, so it is with Christ. For by one Spirit we were all baptized into one body—Jews or Greeks, slaves or free—and all were made to drink of one Spirit. . . . Now you are the body of Christ and individually members of it. (1 Cor. 12:12-13, 27)

This new people carries a living tradition. It carries a tradition because this people lives by virtue of a memory handed down, the memory of Jesus Christ, whose servant love discloses the realm in which sin is no longer the last word of life. This tradition lives—it is much more than a vivid, treasured memory—and the transmission of its occurs in a way that goes beyond a mere handing down:

> We were buried therefore with him by baptism into death, so that as Christ was raised from the dead by the glory of the Father, we too might walk in newness of life. (Rom. 6:4)

Thus God touches the human captivity to sin, releasing response to graciousness.

The Servant of God, furthermore, has an impact on external limitations, those boundaries that are outside the person. The sequence of crucifixion-resurrection-Lord reverberates among the principalities and powers of the world. Among these powers of state, institutions, forceful tradition, and social forces were those that crucified Jesus. The people representing these powers thought that they would stamp him out, but it was not so. The resurrection means that the servant power of God could not be confined or suppressed by the powers, that this divine life was not extinguished either by the death they put him to or by death itself. So Peter formulated the pivot of his sermon at Pentecost: "But God raised him up, having loosed the pangs of death, because it was not possible for him to be held by it" (Acts 2:24).

The consequences were enormous. One consequence concerns Christ himself. He could not be thought of as a privatized, religious, sectarian leader, or as the sponsor of a merely personalized religion, whether of a new line or a rejuvenation of the old. He was a figure of an entirely different order, a solitary One engaged with the elemental forces of life. In his time these forces were manifested in the state, temple, law, and tradition, but these were quickly understood to be manifestations of powers and principalities present everywhere in shifting ways. The sequence of crucifixion-resurrection-Lord made it clear that Christ stood on the edge of life that was defined by these powers, and that he did so in the form of the Servant of God.

A second consequence concerns the powers. They were obviously not done away with, but they were, in a picturesque word, "disarmed," made ineffective, and in that sense destroyed.[2] They were subjected to a great exposé, a costly effort of investigative reporting on the boundaries of life which put the powers in their place. Christ exposed the fact that the power of the powers is an illusion; he thrust a devastating realism on the capacity of the powers to create the illusion of their own supremacy. Hendrik Berkhof writes:

> Where the Spirit of Christ rules, Mammon shrivels down to "finances," conventional morality to a set of rules of thumb, subject to criticism and limited in scope and authority. Changing customs, slogans, and isms of the moment are seen as ideas which are merely "in the air," worth no more and no less than the older slogans they replaced. There the victorious kingship of Christ is confessed, there prevails a consistent unbelief in the utility of military power, and national or international armament is at the most grudgingly accepted as a bitter duty of responsible citizenship. Anxiety before the fearsome future gives way to a simple carefulness, since we know that the future as well is in God's hands.[3]

This suggests liberation, which is the third consequence of Christ's life. The early Christians felt freedom in everyday affairs, as was indicated by the question in Colossians: "If with Christ you died to the elemental spirits of the universe, why do you live as if you still belonged to the world? Why do you submit to regulations, 'Do not handle, Do not taste, Do not touch' " (Col. 2:20–21). This liberation from the nuisance of customary "don'ts" was not simply a device of convenience; it was part of the freedom that produced opposition from local interests and jail sentences and martyrdom for the Christians. This liberation gave evidence that a new way of life had been set loose.

One Sunday, in the summer of 1964, the church I pastored in Rochester, New York, was full. Earlier that week, racial violence had erupted. A team from the Southern Christian Leadership Conference had come to Rochester and Andrew Young, an SCLC member, preached to us. There was a scattering of Blacks throughout the congregation, but mostly there were Whites: confused, angry, fearful, defensive, anguished. Andrew Young told the congregation the story—the story of Jesus, of the SCLC, of Martin Luther King and the struggles. I remember particularly the story of the beach at St. Augustine, Florida. The police, their dogs, the fire hoses and the fear. The commitment and the trust in the only power King and his colleagues had.

Martin Luther King and his colleagues demonstrated many things. Of them, I believe the most important to be that we need not fear or be ruled by the powers of this world, for they have been disarmed. Vision, hope, freedom, and power are ours for the asking. Scripture does not say that the sequence of Christ's life has wiped the powers out, any more than the powers wiped him out. Scripture says that when we meet the powers at the edge of life, on whatever beach we may land, there we may find not only the powers anxious to rule, even to oppress, but also the graciousness of God. Scripture says that so far as we then trust in the sequence of Christ, so far as we open the heart, the mind, and the soul of the Spirit which enables us to participate in that sequence, we then discover we are not captive to the powers but liberated from them.

The deeper one goes into Scripture the more impossible it is to break it up into components. One thing leads into another, so that everything becomes inseparable. The trust that enables one to break through the compulsion of sin cannot be separated from the trust that disarms the powers. If the trust that says "yes" to overcoming sin is withheld from life's encounter with the powers, the "yes" becomes corrupted, and vice versa. If the two are separated, violence is done to both.

Similarly, the trust that leads beyond sin and beyond the powers is the same as the trust creatures have in the Creator. Even so, there is a sense in which the recognition of the Creator and the acceptance of creatureliness is a final act of trust. Israel's faith, as we noted in chapter 12, moved from knowledge of the Redeemer to recognition of the Creator. The dramatic New Testament association of Jesus with creation registers a climax of the same faith.[4] Trust in Christ involved acceptance of being decisively created, of being a creature, of being radically aware of the power and absoluteness of God, and, in an ultimate way, of being dependent upon God.

I have known a moment of total fear only once in my life. In the early autumn of 1945, a hurricane struck New York City. I waited too long before leaving a meeting in Manhattan to get to my wife and our first baby in Queens. By the time the long subway ride was over, the hurricane was upon us. The bus at the end of the subway departed reluctantly, with only a few on it. When it came to my stop, I was the last passenger remaining on the bus, and the driver said he was not going to go further. A ten-minute walk remained for me. It was unnaturally dark. The wind showed what "hurricane force" meant: trees came down; branches were blown around; telephone poles fell and wires snapped, electricity flashing from their loose ends; rain came in blinding, stinging force. An instinct drove me to run along the flower beds, shrubs, and porches of the houses, close in, and to dash across driveways to the next house. I arrived home unhurt, shaking, stricken by an experience of utter fear, a nameless fear in reaction to the wild force of nature's power, a fear for which I was unprepared.

I had no great religious experience during the hurricane or as a result of it, but it did give me a way of understanding what it means to be a creature. Creatureliness evokes fear and stimulates the instinct to protect oneself and survive. One scarcely needs to remark that fear—of hunger, exposure, disease, discomfort, attack, destruction—either makes one sodden or drives one to achieve protection, even independence, from these threats. These are creature fears, and their cure we call creature comforts. In our time the burst of scientific and technological knowledge has escalated comforts and fears to the point where the comforts of some may be impossible to maintain and the fears of all have reached apocalyptic proportions. Creatureliness provides its own limits: the quest of the creature for autonomy increases fear, and these feed upon each other.

To this New Testament experience replies that the fear of being a creature, whether latent or aroused, is dispelled by trust in the Creator. That, however, is not a trust in the adequacy of great machinery of the creation. Rather, it is trust inspired by the rhythms that accompany the action of God-in-Christ. There are two rhythms in the action. We have spoken of one: the sequence of crucifixion-resurrection-Lord. That, however, is set in a grander rhythm which has within it the resonance of the voice of God. Nothing was made, says John, without the Word, and the Word was with God and the Word was made flesh. Christ, says Paul, was in the form of God and emptied himself and took on human form. Does it go too far to say that in that rhythm God became a creature? If that is too much, surely in that rhythm God acknowledges what it means to be a creature and shows the true form of creaturely life. Trust in and obedience to the Creator gives status, dignity, and future to the creature, otherwise confined by servility and fear. The grand rhythm of God-in-Christ implies trust that security in the creation is won by yielding autonomy to obedience. Thus the creature participates in the harmony of God:

> For he has made known to us in all wisdom and insight the mystery of his will, according to his purpose which he set forth in Christ as a plan for the fulness of time, to unite all things on earth. (Eph. 1:9–10)

The spirituality of reenactment, of being "in Christ," introduces those who trust to an ever-new world. On the dark side, sin has a way of erupting and entrapping us in unaccustomed ways. The powers beguile us with the benefits they bestow upon our comfort, or our security, or our need for power. Then they turn with fury to dominate, deny, and corrupt what they have bestowed. The "whole creation" groans ominously under attacks made upon it by a humanity bent upon demonstrating its autonomy.

In the lost condition of humanity, however, these constant elements of darkness are also a source of the new. They are points of entry to the offerings of God. When, driven by the erosions of sin, the battering of the powers, or the anxious striving of creaturely life, one finally acknowledges the limits of human capacities, a new realm opens. It is not the sort of realm that, after a time, becomes old. Even a dim, distant glimpse affords the knowledge that it is a world of undreamt possibilities. The dimensions of our heavy limitations give clues, but only beginning clues, to what lies beyond them in the scarcely imaginable dimensions of freedom in the realm of God.

From this perspective, Christian spirituality may be described as the quality of spirit developed in the process of finding oneself and going home, trusting in the Father's welcome. From the inner reenactment comes new sensitivity to the corrupting pressures of life, while "new mercies, each returning day, hover around us as we pray."[5] The tension between these two poles in human life increases, to be resolved again and again. On the homeward journey one is forgiven and empowered. We are not asked, in the first instance, to adopt principles, espouse values, or promulgate ideas. We are asked to turn from our worlds and enter the kingdom of God, and we are promised that we can do that. Furthermore, we discover, as the people of Scripture discovered, that when the new world of God has been disclosed and we have entered it and it has entered us, we have work to do on earth.

Part IV

SPIRITUALITY: BEING AND DOING, UNITED

The subject of this final part is mission. According to Scripture, mission is not something added on or consciously engaged in by some and not by others, but is rather the outcome of all Christian spirituality, the product when being and doing are united.

So far we have discussed two aspects of Christian spirituality, each of which implies or needs the other. One is the spirituality that requires a transformed sense of identity, the "real me" found in Christ. An exclusive emphasis upon identity, however, would overpsychologize spirituality and would run the danger of vagueness or of anguished, if not paralyzing, introspection. The second aspect of spirituality concerns humanity: humanity lost without God because of the darkness created by inherent human limitations, and humanity found by God in the breakthrough visible in the servant act of Christ. The process of following Christ, of moving from lost to found, entails reenactment of the servant act. In this act the person finds in Christ an objective reference for the new sense of identity and achieves freedom from captivity to the limits of darkness. Even so, this reenactment also runs the danger of being corrupted. In this case one danger is shallow moralism, the mistaken belief that some aspect of moral achievement is the equivalent of "dying daily"; another is the danger of taking the exaltation of a momentary "spiritual high" as authentic rebirth. Both identity and reenactment need each other; both concern the being of the Christian life.

Taken alone identity and reenactment do not convey the full biblical substance and tone. Scripture reaches to the internal depths, but it does not permit one to wallow in them. It summons one beyond introspection to a high calling, to a life for all, to a mission which does not follow the route of messianic illusions or moralistic pride but embarks on a different route. The New Testament pages reverberate with the doing of the Christian life, with its mission, even as they speak of the being of that life. The reason is that in its biblical sense the being contains an urge for the doing and the doing forces a return to the being.

127

16

Mission to Peoples with Concern for Persons

The context of Christian mission is the presence of God among the peoples of humanity. Among these peoples—past, present, and future—and amid all their growth, decay, renewal, and mutations, the divine reality is present—in, behind, and in front of it all—ceaselessly creating community. This active presence of God has been there since the beginning, since time immemorial, prior to Israel, prior to the historical existence of the church, and prior to the arrival of the church among any of the peoples at any time. Presence is prior to covenant.[1]

That insistent theme of Scripture sets the stage for the mission of Christian spirituality. This theme means that the covenant—from the covenant with ancient Israel to the covenant in Christ which constitutes the church—is set within the universal presence and activity of God. God's presence among the peoples of humanity did not cease when the covenant with Israel came into being, and it did not cease when the church was constituted.

As a consequence, Scripture does not depict either Israel or the church as the exclusive funnel of the graciousness of God into the world. The church is not the bearer of God among the peoples in the sense that without the church God is not there; the church does not take God or take Christ to the peoples. Although the church is perforce concerned with the unbelief of peoples, their unbelief, or "paganism," is not the primary context of the church's mission among them. Moreover, the church is not a self-constituted association of persons united by sociological, political, economic, cultural, or moral objectives for the nation or world. These objectives are also its concern, but they do not provide the primary context of its mission. Furthermore, the church does not have a mission because of pride in its faith, and it does not have a sense of superiority because it has the truth or an ideology that claims to have a better worldview than others. The church is not properly a triumphalist, aggressive institution out to remake society on its own terms. The church is not the result of human achievement; it is not formed by lining up on the side of God. In the scriptural view, none of these form the primary and true context of the church's mission, however prominent they may have been or still are in the life of the institutional church. The true context is the universal presence of God with all peoples.

In this context the church has a task and Christian spirituality a thrust. Scripture records the experience of being chosen or called, an experience which comes upon human beings, usually if not always, in an unexpected, surprising way. Touched by God, people make a transfer, sometimes abruptly, from one vehicle to another in their spiritual journey. When they are chosen to enter a new peoplehood, the rhythm of life changes and a new drama takes place, one that is enacted for the sake of all. Therein is the key.

"All," or "for all," is a New Testament code word for the servant act of God in Christ.[2] The direction of the act is outward, toward the peoples among whom God is everywhere present; the character of the act is the obedient but not arrogant, firm but not aggressive quality of the servant. Participation in the act—transfer to the new peoplehood—results in a constant posture and action of testimony to the One who binds them together. That is the task. Chosen to participate in the servant act, Christians present testimony to the Servant of God, to Christ the Lord, to God-in-Christ. This testimony, when it eschews arrogance and exhibits the qualities of the servant, shows the way to an open door, to the way by which God's graciousness breaks through the oppressiveness of life's limits. Such testimony to the peoples shows the way to the presence already there.[3]

Obviously, such a mission puts a high premium upon the quality of life of those who engage in it. Scripture clearly demands authenticity in the household of God. The people of Scripture also knew that falsity is a plague of the faithful. One reason lies in the process entailed by the new life. Baptism signifies a movement from one people to another;

the Christian life is a transformation of one principle of peoplehood by another. This process means that, because the church has drawn its membershp from the surrounding people, the characteristics of that people are imported into its life, as we know from the behavior of those in Corinth and Colossae on down to the present. Herein is a fundamental "catch twenty-two" in the mission of the church. The more success the church achieves in its mission, the more it takes into itself the tenacious peoplehood which surrounds it. As we noted in chapter 9, this sometimes produces a terrible distortion, so that Christianity becomes more a part of the enduring problem of Christian spirituality than a solution to it. In any case, the need for continued achievement of inner rebirth becomes a primary part of mission, lest the salt lose its savor (Matt. 5:13). This endemic need for the renewal of the church and the validation of its message affects each of the three aspects of mission to which we now turn.

The experience of being bound together by the self-emptying servant act of God-in-Christ produces a particular sensitivity to and care for one's own people and those throughout the world. From this a mission of concerned watching and warning comes to expression. This was suggested long ago in stirring words, in the pain and bewilderment of a bitter exile, when the people was no more:

> So you, son of man, I have made a watchman for the house of Israel; whenever you hear a word from my mouth, you shall give them warning from me. . . . Say to them, As I live, says the Lord God, I have no pleasure in the death of the wicked, but that the wicked turn from his way and live; turn back, turn back from your evil ways; for why will you die, O house of Israel? (Ezek. 33:7, 11; compare 3:17)

The theme of "watching" lies deep in Scripture. In one sense all the authors of Scripture are watchers, first warning Israel, then the church, and always the world, taking no delight in wickedness but never fearful of exposing it, holding forth the presence of God. Moses watched over the tribes. The prophets issued warnings. Ezekiel acknowledged a specific appointment to be a watchman, a part of his function as prophet, given by God. Jesus spoke of watchfulness for the kingdom of God, warning us lest we be unprepared.

This watching and warning of peoples is accompanied by particular concern for the person. Ezekiel possessed a compassion for the individual which exceeded even the compassion of Jeremiah. God's presence in Ezekiel's unprecedented, desperate situation of the exile made it clear that no disorder of people could cut the person off from God. Hard but not harsh, the warning included care for the person; it gave people a chance to turn. Ezekiel foreshadows the New Testament in this matter;[4] the exhortation, pleading, and encouragement spoken of and offered in the name of Christ include the same care of God for the individual:

> Blessed be the God and Father of our Lord Jesus Christ, the Father of mercies and God of all comfort, who comforts us in all our affliction, so that we may be able to comfort those who are in any affliction, with the comfort with which we ourselves are comforted by God. (2 Cor. 1:3–4)

Perhaps the tones of warning and assurances of comfort are nowhere more forcefully blended than in Jesus' announcement: "the kingdom of God is at hand; repent, and believe in the gospel" (Mark 1:14). That announcement provides the true note of the church's mission of warning to peoples; issued in the Spirit of God, the warning includes the cure of souls.[5]

What is to be watched and warned against? Two concerns emerge.[6]

The first is the extent to which a people is captive to the limits that stand between humans and God. One may reflect that a people is hardly ever entirely captive to these limits, that God's presence operates in spite of them, creating the community, the peoplehood, necessary for life. Even so, the limitations to human existence continue, blinding humans to God's presence, thwarting God's purpose. Therefore, the question, To what extent is a people—our people—captive? is always pertinent. Captivity may result from a people's failure to be aware of limitations and to perceive their importance; people may live in darkness and not know it. Thus the warning of the church to the people has a caring, even educational aspect: to make clear that a people (not only individuals) may sin, that a people may become subject to the powers within it, that a people may disregard its relation to creation. Captivity, however, may also be more sinister than mere ignorance. A people may embrace the things that hold them captive. We Americans, for instance, are good at producing things, and we like the things we produce. However, we are captive to this affection when the result is a genuine materialism which elevates things to the point where they dominate us. That is a form of worshiping the creature—a captivity which stands between us and the Creator. Another way the creature is worshiped is when a race is worshiped, as did Josiah Strong and the Nazis. And there are so many other ways. In biblical terms people not only live in darkness; they love it. This is the depth of the church's warning.

At times this warning becomes strident. Nearly all of the traditions of Scripture record acute stress. When peoples are too heavily captive to life's limits, the warnings take on an absolute quality. When the Tower of Babel was built too high, when the people wanted to return to Egypt, when Israel's neighbors committed heinous crimes, when Job insisted too hard upon his righteousness, when Israel itself transgressed too greatly, when Jesus identified his ministry, when peoples were judged callous toward the thirsty, the hungry, and the imprisoned, the warnings came down hard. Such warnings communicate the prospect of disaster: peoples go too far. Failings gain momentum, become virtually irreversible, and make recovery or renewal next to impossible. To be sure, one would draw this to a fine point or become dogmatic about it only at peril. Scripture communicated danger to peoples by urgency of tone and language, not by explicit theory; but that accentuates the serious possibility of disaster for the people. That such extreme trouble may come upon the people is part of the church's warning, not to be issued lightly lest those who speak for it falsely cry "wolf." When the organized life of the church transgresses these limits, the warning is severe.[7]

The second concern that Scripture watches over is the integrity of the people and its peoplehood. As noted in chapter 5, Scripture contains a test of a people's integrity: Does the operative principle of the peoplehood in question work to deny peoplehood to some or create it for all? Thus Scripture returns again and again to the dispossessed, its passionate concern becoming a dominant theme. The contemporary world rightly. puts this concern in terms of human rights Scripture perceives that human rights are provided or denied by the bond that actually unites a people, and it directs attention to the adequacy of the peoplehood (whichever one it may be) to provide for them. When those rights are denied, when a people dispossesses other people or a portion of its own population by aggression, neglect or exclusion, the watching function of the church leads it to make a warning. This warning goes to the roots of human life. In scriptural perspective the dispossessed are the result or consequence of a flaw in the bond that unites the people, a flaw in peoplehood, its operating principle. The warning is aroused by the plight of the dispossessed; it is directed to the character of the people and its uniting principles. And when a church itself participates in or acquiesces to this most acute form of corruption, it becomes the object of warning. " 'I hate, I despise your feasts, and I take no delight in your solemn assemblies' " (Amos 5:21).

The first part of Christian mission to peoples is to watch and warn; the second is to participate in the renewal of peoples. Obviously, the question of how this is to be done has been debated throughout the church's history. In our present time this debate is intense,[8] and it points to the underlying issue, namely, the character of a people, Scripture's bottom line in this respect. (See chapter 5.) This scriptural concern for a people's character is so important that it forms the basis for a further aspect of the church's mission to peoples. That mission calls the church to participate in the life of the surrounding people by urgently raising an important question and by collaborating in discovering answers to it.

We may call this the prophetic question, because it is indirectly suggested by the prophetic tradition of Scripture. As the prophets directed their message to the fidelity and character of Israel's people, and as Jesus directed his kingdom message toward all people, so Christians may question the fidelity and character of the people among whom they live. One formulation of the question is, simply, What kind of people do we want to be? That question may also take these forms: What sense of human identity do we wish to possess? In what creativity do we wish to engage? What character do we wish to exhibit? Each of these questions is a needed, far-reaching form of the basic question.

Our society is frequently referred to as being part of Western technological society, which, doubtlessly is accurate. But, taking thought, one wonders whether—if we had had any choice in the matter—we would have chosen that identity. What of values and the finer qualities of life? The West is known for them, but chiefly so? The current debate in the United States over "secular humanism" raises questions about human values and their source, and is a phase of a longstanding discussion concerning the relation of the Christian faith to them.[9] By what type of creativity should we want to be recognized? What creativity and culture should properly arise from love of neighbor, from the acceptance and critique of culture, and from response to nature? Further, the rugged individualism, the openness, the violence, the friendliness, and now the narcissism and hedonism of the American character have all been evident at one time or another or in one aspect or another of society. Can a people long afford to let these issues of character go unattended? And how can concern for them be related to the need for pluralism? What relation, in other words, should unity and freedom have in our society?

When the question is seriously asked, the object is the bond that unites the people. What kind of people do we want to be? does not refer, if asked in a scriptural sense, to individuals, except indirectly. The question goes beyond individuals to the bond that unites them because that bond, written with individual variation upon the inward parts of each person (see chapter 6), is crucial for the corporate people and the persons within it. In this way the bond of peoplehood is prior to any particular issues of character or of policy that appear among the people. In the United States, for instance, we are at present heavily issue oriented, but—even though specific issues should be kept in mind—primary attention should be directed toward the people as a whole and toward the bond that unites them. In this way the true priority emerges. The question then becomes, What kind of bond should unite us and how does it relate to specific problems?

A company of black men and women was discussing the relation of men and women in the black church and community.[10] They said the issue of sexism is no more resolved with them than it is among Whites. Their approach, however, was governed by an overall concern. These people had in mind the needs of the black community, their struggle for survival, their absolute need for justice. In this plight, they said, black men and women need each other. The problems of sexism need to be resolved so that the black church and black community are strengthened. With their attention fixed upon an issue and a people, this group focused upon the true priority: How can the bond between black men and women be changed so as to strengthen the bond that unites black people? In all of this discussion, the broader question was present both explicitly and implicitly. They perceived that black commitment to justice, the struggle for justice resulting from that commitment, and the achievement of their goal would contribute to and enrich the people of the United States and the bond that unites them. Thus, two contemporary issues—sexism and racism—were each treated in a biblical spirit, not as mere issues of self-interest, but as aspects of peoplehood, both black and American.

The question, What kind of a people do we want to be? must be asked persistently and vigorously. When a people is in trouble and decay, the problems of security occupy people's minds, and security consciousness, not character, is primary. When the people is on an upward turn of nation building, the momentum of triumph and aggrandizement may be at the fore, with questions of character submerged by the sense of power. When a vast mutation in the peoplehood is in progress, the excitement and bewilderment of change directs attention to the self, overtaking concern for the collective character. When there is revolution, the need for victory is primary, with issues of character postponed or relegated to the doctrine underlying the revolution. When peaceful development is both possible and in progress, attention is given primarily to the relation between steps taken now and future goals, and character takes second place behind technique. In these or other conditions, the mission of Christian spirituality requires persistence and vigor in raising the question, What kind of a people do we wish to be?

The question, moreover, also implies that it be asked in an informed fashion. Obviously, technical issues and the issues of peoplehood strongly affect one another. Science and technology raise issues of their uses in war and peace; the organization and functioning of the economy affects well-being; communications influence relationships and the speed of change—and so on. These alone suggest that the character of a people is not—if indeed it ever was—a simple moral issue, to be settled merely by making people good. The character of a people presents a complex problem. To raise the question, What kind of people do we wish to be? with effect requires information, insight, and the capacity to use both.

The question must be put vigorously. It must be raised in an informed manner, and it must be asked with strategy. Indeed, Christian spirituality possesses its own sense as to what is strategically important. This strategy is not based upon prudent calculation of self-interest, although this must come into play, or upon estimates of timing and the strategy of success, although these may also have a role. Scripture yields different starting points and suggests its own strategy. What kind of people do we wish to be? should be asked at the points where the limits of life have impact upon the people and where their influence crisscrosses in the life of people. This requires reflection and analysis, aided by every relevant form or discipline of human knowledge. The strategy is to ask the question at these crowded ways of life. The limits are never merely abstract, but always specific. One aspect of Christian spirituality is the capacity to discern how they operate within and affect a specific people. For us that means we should try to perceive how the limits show up in the American people and its relationships with other peoples.

To watch and to warn, to raise questions vigorously, persistently, and with an informed strategy about the character of the surrounding people imply further participation by Christians in the people's life. The impact of the question, What kind of people do we wish to be? is itself participatory. Sincerely asked by Christians and the church, it avoids telling our neighbors what our collective character as a people in the United States ought to be and, instead, invites their thought concerning it. In a questioning frame of mind, most Christians will discover neighbors who do not embrace the church and who ask our own question about the peoplehood in a more penetrating manner than we do. A questioning attitude also implies that, at the minimum, some fragment of an answer will be discovered, and this leads to debate, negotiation, and settlement of the issue—at least for the time being and in a provisional way.[11]

Whenever there is pluralism in society, "negotiation" may be the crucial symbolic word for Christian participation in people formation. Not long ago an interracial group was engaged in vigorous discussion about racial justice in the United States.[12] David Ramage, a white person with long experience in community organizing, and another person, also white, were speaking. "But the Blacks don't want Whites to be 'nice' to them," Ramage said. "Blacks want Whites to negotiate

with them for a just piece of the pie." The Blacks in the meeting
agreed; Ramage had expressed an essential quality of the negotiating
stance, and, indirectly, a symbol of Christian action in society.

Negotiation implies not only a stance and posture of respect but a
strategy in relation to power. One aspect of this strategy is the creation
of power. Negotiation stimulates the creation of power among the
powerless, for negotiation is empty unless there is someone to
negotiate with. Thus labor created its own power base in the thirties;
Blacks began to do so in the sixties; and women in the seventies
(preceded by the struggle for the vote). The symbol of negotiation
requires the effort to create the base for negotiation. Furthermore,
negotiation gives constructive point to the various techniques of confrontation. Confrontation, while at times essential, in itself only goes
partway; its effective purpose comes clear when it leads to negotiation.[13]

So understood, negotiation requires that conflicting interests be
brought together. The art of negotiation lies in discovering mutual
interests that can be satisfied by agreement. The effectiveness of
negotiation lies not just in achieving an agreement but in negotiating
interests that are related to power. The agreement then has weight. In
our present situation many Christians well appreciate the uses of power
and use participation in the political process as a license to secure their
own viewpoints by political action. Negotiation, however, is not a
license to use power to put across one's own interests. Instead, negotiation calls forth the use of imagination to perceive mutual interests
among those who need to gain power and among those who hold
power. It also calls forth the determination to stay with the negotiating
process until agreement is reached. Thus, Christians who negotiate in
this sense can be open, using imagination but also welcoming the
imagination of others, advancing their concerns and interests but
appreciating those of others—always seeking common ground. And if
common ground cannot be found? Pray, and keep trying.

Negotiation as a strategy in the process of peoplehood formation
requires a broad range of specific negotiating action. If negotiation
may best be done around a conference table, untold numbers of
conference tables—in all sorts of families, neighborhoods, communities, occupations, institutions, structures, and in all kinds of life

processes throughout society—should be brought into action and, perhaps, many new ones should be created. It may happen that U.S. society will call forth increasingly strident warnings, that the question, What kind of people do we wish to be? will arise with growing urgency, and that participation in the renewal of the American peoplehood will be inescapable. If this transpires, many occasions and many conference tables will be needed, and the problems will be urgent.

Actually, I believe that this moment is at hand. Perhaps the most banal remark to be made about present-day society is that it is in transition. The appearance of banality, however, can be a ruse of the devil, for transition of the scope we now experience comes to a momentous shift in our peoplehood and, consequently, in our identity as a people. That touches the fundamentals of life itself.

This identity, this peoplehood, this community, gives means and hope to life itself. The health and vigor of the human sense of identity depend upon a constructive relationship between the core of the individual and the core of the communal culture. The hope of keeping the vast powers, which are endemic to all societies, in their proper place in our society lies in the character of the peoplehood. The hope of responding constructively to the pressures of fear, to the inflated desire for security, and to futile efforts to establish our autonomy in the world of neighbors and of nature lies in the character of the peoplehood.

To ignore the problem of our peoplehood would be to turn away from the very quality of community that makes life possible and worthwhile and to open the door to rampant self-worship. To retreat to sectional, economic, ethnic, moral, or other enclaves of self-interest would be to give the whole over to domination by the structures and processes of power. To give into fear would raise security interests to the status of a god, which, like the Ba'al of old, will be asleep in the hour of need.

To these and related tendencies, Christian spirituality replies "no." Because of inherent concern for persons, Christian spirituality turns to the people and its peoplehood: to warn, to question, and to participate in the work of people formation.

17

Mission to Persons in Awareness of Peoplehood

In the providence of God, Christian mission today takes place within two distinct historical situations. First, a growing people consciousness on a global scale increasingly provides the historical context of mission. One would overstate the matter if one claimed that this consciousness is wholly new. It is not. Biblical faith arose amid the shifting peoples of the eastern Mediterranean world and, in spite of periods of stagnation, those committed to Christian mission have been ever aware of their task among different peoples. Nevertheless, contemporary people-consciousness is different because it is also global in fact; it thus presents a totality of the world's cultures and peoples to each people and, in astounding measure, to each person in the same historical moment.

Second, Christian mission today takes place also in the consciousness of a parallel movement in the church itself. The latter has also become worldwide in fact, the twentieth century being the first time this has been true. For most of its history, with some exceptions in Asia and Africa, Christianity has been largely European, with the United States-Canadian offshoot. One aspect of the history of Christianity, however, has been its expansion.[1] Today, the church is in fact worldwide and growing, and it is being anticipated that by the turn of the century the majority of Christians will for the first time be found among the peoples of the Southern Hemisphere.[2] This has produced a rapidly intensifying people-consciousness in Christianity, as the Christian gospel has become indigenous to these various peoples. Instead of the business suit and housedress, Christianity is now beginning—

albeit slowly—to appear in a marvelous variety of styles and colors. For the discharge of mission, this means that no longer is mission something done by one people (the European/American) for another; but that the church within each people has its own mission, and that when help is needed, other churches among other peoples join—upon invitation.

The development of global people-consciousness generally and in the church specifically is made possible by scientific technology of highly ambiguous impact. A symbol of this ambiguity is that the majority of major scientific and technological developments of the modern era were first achieved in wartime.[3] Moreover, the people consciousness of our contemporary period has been brought about less by peaceful, cultural interchange than by the interplay of imperialisms, revolutions, reactions, and wars. If one welcomes the growth of global people-consciousness, one recognizes that it is not marked by clear virtue but by ambiguity.

These developments have significant consequences for Christian mission. The observable character of the church and our everyday experience of the church are undergoing decisive change. The church no longer bears witness to its universal vision primarily within Western civilization and hence in the cultural and social terms of the West, but bears its witness within virtually all societies and peoples. The church is no longer predominantly a part of a white, relatively homogeneous culture but a part of "all people that on earth do dwell," and therefore a part of many cultures that are very different from one another. It is a church groping to conceptualize its identity among peoples everywhere who are searching for their identities, searching in a global process of which no one knows the outcome, save by faith.

In the process, however, one thing seems certain. The church is no one's possession. The white church (meaning all the white denominations) in the United States, for instance, does not belong only to itself; it has been permanently altered—although not fast enough—by Martin Luther King and his predecessors and successors in the black church as well as by the influence of Latin Americans in the United States and in the southern continent. European Christianity has been changed by African and Asian Chrisitanity. The channels of the old imperialism no longer run in the old direction, but they carry new freight in the opposite direction, in the church as well as among the peoples in general. The male church no longer belongs to men. Roman Catholicism, Protestantism, and Orthodoxy influence each other, discuss unity, and in many cases act together. Everywhere the church is changed by the same global people-consciousness which produced the World Council of Churches in 1948 and Vatican II in 1962–65, both of which, rooted in the West, nevertheless clearly understood that they symbolized a people among the peoples.

This twentieth-century development has thus been stimulated by and has helped bring about a renewed biblical consciousness concerning Christian mission. Furthermore, this people-consciousness has been the fertile ground for a renewed appreciation of the pristine hope of Christian faith. In the twentieth-century encounter of people with peoples, Christians have increasingly turned to the biblical hope for the future. Rather than drawing hope from the progress of human achievement, Christians have found again the hope that lies in God's transformation and consummation of human life.

Not only does people consciousness have a continuity with the conditions within which biblical faith arose, it has continuity with the sociology implied in the vision of the people drawn from the peoples recorded in the book of Acts. The book of Acts is introduced not by its sociology but by a statement of the ever new knowledge of faith:

> In the first book, O Theophilus, I have dealt with all that Jesus began to do and teach, until the day when he was taken up, after he had given commandment to the apostles whom he had chose. To them he presented himself alive after his passion by many proofs, appearing to them during forty days, and speaking of the Kingdom of God. (Acts 1:1–3)

This statement expresses the optimism and hope of Christian mission, whether in the Mediterranean culture of Acts or the global consciousness of the twentieth century. The report of Jesus alive after his Passion, speaking of the kingdom of God, does not attest occult mysteries, but reveals the purpose of God. The course of human history is revealed as not vain, but meaningful, not aimless, but purposeful.

From Abraham to the Exodus, and from the Exodus to Christ, God's promise defines the future, and Scripture breathes the conviction that the promise carries power. The people heard the promise of a new land as more than a mere forecast that they would somehow or another get out of Egypt. The promise inspired the conviction that God would "bring to effect what he had promised in the deliverance of the people from bondage."[4] In Scripture promise becomes purpose.

This knowledge of a divine future produced the supreme affirmation of biblical faith. The climactic promise that the kingdom of God will come transformed the early perception of the future. The promise of the kingdom of God is like the Exodus promise in that it contains a deliverance from bondage. It is unlike the Exodus promise in the sense that Jesus does not lead a people to approach a distant land; rather, he enables people to enter a realm of life which approaches them. As Jesus taught, the kingdom of God is not a place. It consists of recast values, transfigured relationships, and unimaginable dimensions of life in the Divine Presence, none of which can be simply relegated to the future but are here now, yet cannot be encompassed in the present for they are still to come. The kingdom of God is not merely a good option for the future; it is the future that God has fashioned for humanity. It is the reality of present and future that Jesus announced and into which he leads those who will follow:

> For he has made known to us in all wisdom and insight the mystery of his will, according to his purpose which he set forth in Christ as a plan for the fulness of time, to unite all things in him, things in heaven and things on earth. (Eph. 1:9–10)

Scripture invites trust in God's plan for the future. The optimism thereby implied, however, does not rest upon progress in the sense of reaching a goal on an ascending plane of effort throughout human history, generation after generation, civilization after civilization. Nor is this optimism based upon the spread of Christianity among the world's peoples, as if that would produce a Christian world. The kingdom of God requires human testimony to its presence and to its coming, but it does not emerge from the progress of human or ecclesiastical achievement. The kingdom of God does not come "with signs to be observed" (Luke 17:21).

On the contrary, Scripture understands the self to be subject to inherent limitations which even—especially?—creativity cannot escape. In Scripture's view of history, these limits, not creativity, occupy center stage. The witness and mission of the church on a global scale provide a more universal testimony as to the nature of human limits and God's breakthrough of them. It is testimony for all, more adequately fulfilling the spirit of the Servant because it is so. Moreover, the context of global realities and consciousness lends unusual urgency to the mission. In this global village of peoples and of powers, the limits are writ large and clear and in terrifying language. If human autonomy in respect of the natural world has reached such proportions as to make it theoretically possible to disrupt the biosphere; if the mushroom of human achievement has reached so high as to bring about the scorched decimation of earth and its inhabitants; if oppression stunts whole populations; and if the principalities of states, corporations, ideologies, armaments, financial structures, and other arrays of the powers of this world seem to be all but uncontrollable—then the testimony to God's power to break through these limits carries an urgency that would be unbearable if God had not also made it liberating. Trust in that breakthrough of God, trust in Jesus' announcement, descriptions, and demonstration of the kingdom of God produces its own optimism as to the course and destiny of human life.

This optimism results from the knowledge, imparted by faith, that ultimately life and history are gracious, that God will bring the promised plan to effect in the climax and consummation of human history. This kingdom, however, is not beyond in the sense of another world or something simply in the afterlife or merely in the future. The exalted language of Scripture varies, but it always refers to human life and the world, transformed. Here it is a seed which, planted, appears as a wondrous growth. There it is human life reborn, where people have a unity that is like the unity between Jesus and God. Elsewhere it is people transferred from one realm to another, a world reconciled to God, a new creation.[5] All of these things begin now. Based upon God's promise with power built into it, manifest in the reality of Christ, and validated again and again by all to whom the mind of Christ is given, this optimism is founded upon the hope that reaches into the limits of human life and beyond them to the transformation of life.

That hope will not let Christian spirituality alone, to lie fallow. The work of God in the world evokes the response of mission.

But you are a chosen race, a royal priesthood, a holy nation, God's own people, that you may declare the wonderful deeds of him who called you out of darkness into his marvellous light. Once you were no people but

now you are God's people; once you had not received mercy but now you
have received mercy. (1 Pet. 2:9–10)

As presented in the New Testament, the church is never static, but
always dynamic. "You are the body of Christ," says Paul. "I am the
vine, you are the branches," says Jesus as reported by John. "You are a
holy nation" is the phrase from 1 Peter. These descriptions direct
attention primarily to what the church is, to the being of the church,
but the New Testament does not leave it there. A "that" is always
implied: "that the world may believe" in John's Gospel; "that you may
declare" in 1 Peter. The task of the church among the peoples describes the nature of the church as much as the nature of the church
determines its task. The movement of the New Testament spirtuality
comes from uniting the Christian's being in Christ with participation
in the work of Christ. "You are . . . that you may . . ."

The declaration or testimony of the new people among the peoples of
the world has a double function and accent. On the one hand, it acts as
demonstration: it warns, it questions, and it participates in people
formation and renewal. On the other hand, the people in Christ invites
persons into its own peoplehood. Its testimony to God-in-Christ always
carries the note of invitation. Whether this invitation to enter the Body
of Christ be issued directly or indirectly, to people in masses or to
individuals one by one, it is never casual. The church is called to testify
to the living God and to invite persons and the peoples themselves into
the kingdom of God. This invitation has little to do with the member-
ship of an institution; it has to do with God. How and where, then, is it
to be issued? How and where may the church discharge its mission to
persons? To these questions Scripture yields an answer, but it is one of
substance, not of technique; or, rather, in reply to these questions
Scripture provides a substantial answer which frees imagination to
develop technique.

Our house in central Minnesota, well within its woodland tract,
stands upon the shoulder of a small but definite rise, the land dropping
away to the west and sharply rising above the shoulder to the east.
From the small parking area a driveway runs down to where it all levels
out to a road. The house and driveway were newly constructed, and,
toward the end of our first summer, in 1975, torrential rains made it

clear that before the next summer the parking area and driveway would need to be rebuilt. This was done, using granite chip, a super-gravel resulting from the famous granite of this part of the state. Although it had been expertly laid down, the new driveway only partly solved the problem. Further rains showed that adequate drainage required various contours in the gravel surface, leading in different directions. With a garden rake I began a long period of careful grading, now here, now there; on hands and knees sighting out the result; standing in rainstorms and watching the channels; regrading; and then doing it all over the next time. Finally it was complete, and it remains, no matter what torrents of rain the sudden thunderstorms produce. I learned a valuable lesson from this experience: not only does water flow downhill, but water has its own sense of matter of which—as I graded, watched in the rain, and regraded—I became acutely aware. The feel of water for downhill was different from my sight of downhill. The flow corrected my sight, and my efforts with rake and gravel had to bend to the water.

So the grace of God flows in its own ways, different from our view of them. The objective of Christian mission to persons among the world's peoples is to help them discover the channels of God's grace, to discover how and where it flows.

What are these channels? More precisely, at what points in human experience do the downhill channels begin? The preceding chapters have suggested that according to biblical experience God becomes known to human beings in relation to certain aspects of their condition as human beings. Those whom God found discovered that they had been touched at identifiable points, beyond which as human beings they had not been able to reach by their own efforts, but at which God's presence broke through to them. If, like Job, or like the rich young man confronting Jesus (Matt. 19:16–22; Mark 10:17–22; Luke 18:18–23), one conducts one's own search, looking for God at the points in life where one supposes God is or wishes God to be, the result may be surprising: not there, but at the points that stand between Me and you. These function as limits, not theoretical but actual limits upon human life. While they can be discerned in everyday life, it would be a mistake to impose or try too strenuously to discover a neat system in them.

Human limits as envisaged in Scripture have certain things in common. They are constants. Because humans are human, they (1) live as peoples; (2) encounter the fact of creation and their own creatureliness; (3) live among powers and principalities; and (4) are subject to the compulsions of sin. No individual person is exempt from these limitations. Moreover, there is ambiguity, a mixture of good and evil, about each of these constant conditions of human life, except sin. Scripture announces that God created the world and its inhabitants and indicates that peoplehood and the powers are in some sense derived from God. There is good in all. Yet they are also corrupt, or corrupted. Both good and evil, these limits upon our life are ambiguous. Sin is the exception: it was not created by God; it is not good; and it corrupts the whole. Sin is unambiguously bad. Yet sin is not understood save in relation to our creatureliness, or to the corruption of the principalities and powers, or to the people and peoplehood of which they are a part. These limits serve to make sin come alive, in a way analogous to what Paul said about the law: that apart from it he should not have known sin (Rom. 7:7).[6] These limits and their interrelationships stand between humans and God.

Otherwise stated, these limits are the boundaries between the wrath of men and the righteousness of God. The trouble and wrath that really matter, that separate us from God, from neighbor, and from self, come upon us in relation to these limits. Possessing a reflexive, backlash effect, these limits are the source of human wrath. Because this is so, God's love touches us where wrath is felt, where the limits confine, where the boundaries make us desperate or sodden. Graciousness opens. The troubled limits which bore down upon our life become the points at which God's action introduces us to the freedom, righteousness, and salvation which result from recognizing the final limit of all life.

These points define the strategy of Christian mission to persons. The limits that oppress life indicate where the downhill channels of grace flow. So much we know from biblical experience, validated by our own pilgrimage with God. From this point knowledge of contemporary society and life, discernment, the experience of others in the Christian community, and imagination must work together to help others perceive that God exists and has meaning. One asks, however, what form this help may take. So far we have suggested that in substance Christian spirituality comes from the impact of God's graciousness upon the oppressive limits to life. We have then turned this into a strategy for mission: the gospel is preached in reference to those limits, not in a theoretical sense, but specifically, so the people may see the channels in the parking areas and driveways of their own lives and perceive the meaning of God in these ways. This overall strategy, however, requires tactics.

To appreciate the tactics of Christian mission, however, one must recall the drama at the beginning of the Acts of the Apostles. An overpowering intensification of God's presence suddenly impelled the followers of Jesus to go into the surrounding society. Pentecost (Acts 2:1–41) is both symbol and substance of this; the apostolic calling is sign and vehicle, and the response to it is evidence. The overall point can hardly be escaped: the Spirit of God entered that ancient world and created a new situation in it. Furthermore, Acts records that in response the apostles, empowered by this Spirit, themselves entered their surrounding world and created situations in it. The accounts of the preaching, the internal struggles, the encounters, the successes, and the failures that fill the book of Acts record the beginning and the increase of a deep historical turbulence. This Spirit and the gospel penetrated to the roots of life and encompassed its meaning. That was the new historical situation of the apostolic age.

In their work of mission, the apostles and their associates did what had been done to them. God had newly entered their histories, and they entered into the life of their times, filled, as they acknowledged, with the same Spirit. God had created a situation in which they had received a supreme gift. In turn, by their life style, their preaching, their varied activities, and their reaction to opposition, they created situations in which others might receive the same gift.

In this rhythm of entering and creating one discerns the tactics of Christian mission. If the strategy of mission is to present the Gospel in relation to those points where (as we learn from Scripture) humans are held in a constant captivity which separates them from God, the tactic of mission is to enter contemporary situations that express these limits and to create situations where the Holy Spirit may work. This may be further stated as follows:

> The tactic of Christian mission is to enter any situation of life at its critical points, that is, where limits of peoplehood, sin, powers, and creatureliness

hold people captive, in order to create occasions there in which the Holy Spirit may free people from their captivities, and enable them to enter the kingdom and people of God.

In this mission, much, if not everything, depends upon what we have earlier called reenactment. (See chapter 15.) The use of the word requires a conscious modesty. The idea or prospect of reenactment of the servant mind of Christ brings pause to the soul, a moment of true humility. We are not Christ. Yet Christ is not so exalted that his act is either removed from us or affects us only by its remote action, as when we merely give assent to the proposition "He died for our sins" or accept the idea that he atoned for them in some merely juridical way. The New Testament boldly demands the kind of participation in the act of God-in-Christ that will make us different persons.

This participation or reenactment has a direct bearing upon Christian mission today. (1) It enables the Christian community and person to *perceive* the contemporary forms of constant human captivities. (2) It produces a *form of action* for mission. (3) It provides a *style* of Christian mission. The remainder of this chapter is concerned with brief enlargements upon these three aspects of Christian mission.

Mission at any time and place requires perception of human need. This perception comes from Christian participation in two things at once. One is our participation in the peoplehood—for us, the layered peoplehood of the United States—which is the matrix of our personal development (see chapter 4) and the precarious context in which we experience the limitations that make us aware of being lost and without God. (See chapters 10—13.) Second, we participate in the Christian community, the people whose bond is God-in-Christ, in which we are developing a new identity and receiving evermore the freedom and life which is beyond the limits of our lostness. The more the Christian community—the persons in it and the community itself—acts, reflects, and prays about this double participation, the clearer its perception becomes. The vivid, concrete, unabashed style of Scripture is, or should be, the guide: what oppresses, limits, and binds persons is not abstract but rather the specific manifestation of those things which in fact hold humans in bondage. Although Scripture shows us the basics of these limits and captivities (see parts II and III), it cannot pinpoint the way they appear in modern society and personal life. For that we Christians need to engage in a sequence of thought, research, discussion, mutual exploration, and prayer. Underneath these, however, lies the crucial factor: the spiritual capacity to discern. A question thus arises concerning our spiritual renewal and our mission:

> Is my [individual] and our [church] participation in and reenactment of the servant act of God-in-Christ of such a quality as to enable us to perceive the specific, contemporary manifestations of the limits that bind human beings?

Perception leads to the second aspect of mission to persons. When we discern we must act. Reenactment not only produces the perception required by Christian mission, it is the motor that drives the action of Christian mission. The quality of life in Christ empowers the Christian community to enter or create situations to the end that people may be enabled to transcend their human captivities. How may we do that? We do not wish here to present a program, for that must be worked out on the spot, situation by situation, occasion by occasion. Here we suggest a symbol and a second question to stimulate the process of program and action.

"Reenactment" is one word primary to Christian mission, and it suggests a further word, also symbolic of action. Many have claimed that the Christian is to present Christ to people. In our culture, however, so much has been said about Christ, denominational and theological differences about Christ have been so acute, that "to present Christ" becomes almost an empty phrase. For a word symbolic of mission today, I turn to David Tracy's language: "re-present Christ."[7] It contains a good pun which implies Paul's "ambassadors of Christ." At the same time it suggests the need to get away from what is not authentic and to recover what is authentic in Christian presentations of Christ. In our culture, How may we re-present Christ? is a different question than How may we present Christ? Moreover, re-present suggests the need for boldness in (1) conserving what is authentic; (2) discarding what is no longer (or ever has been) authentic; and (3) innovating in order to restate what is authentic. To re-present Christ depends upon and draws content from a reenactment which goes to the core of the personal and the core of the communal identity. (See chapter 8.) Thus, the boldness of re-presenting Christ does not call for mere trial-and-error innovation, but for a decisive reaching out to the persons who are troubled, alienated, and held captive within the peoplehood of our time and place. Therefore, a second question arises concerning Christian mission to persons:

> In what manner may the Christian declaration be made within our people and its peoplehood so as to re-present Christ to those persons whose lives are limited by sin, by the powers and principalities, and by creatureliness?

Reenactment produces not only the perception and the representation needed by Christian mission, but it also produces a style of Christian mission. This, we suggest, is most properly a confessional, or confessing, style. The biblical passages from Isaiah, the Gospel of John, and the epistle to the Philippians which appear on p. 110 give the framework of meaning for the words "confessing" and "confessional." Two considerations, however, lie in the background. First, a confessional style is not imperious and dogmatic, although it may give witness to the same truth that dogma seeks to enshrine, nor is it attached in any fashion, direct or indirect, to an attempt to coerce or bribe. Second, a confessional style requires, either directly or indirectly, a declaration made in the first person, in the language of "I believe" or "We believe." Uttered in this style, "I believe" presents a claim as to the truth, but in such a way that the claim itself, or the statement itself, is allowed to carry its own weight and to stand at the center of attention. In this way the three biblical passages show the style of "to confess." The Isaiah passage describes the servant so that it is a statement in itself; the prologue to John's Gospel and the hymn in Philippians each presents an account of Christ which, like other New Testament accounts of Christ, stands in itself and is offered on its own merits. To be sure, Christians unfortunately can misuse these statements: through dogmatic, coercive "we have the truth," "your salvation depends on it" tones and terms; or through bribing terms of "you will have health or happiness or prosperity"; or through esoteric, in-house, mystery religion, institutional language; or through claims that Jesus and God are "good for America" (which they are, but in a different way from what is usually meant and implied). These claims distort the clarity and directness of a confessional style that originates in first-person testimony to God-in-Christ. Finally, a confessing style grows out of the life of the community and the person. What is confessed is an expression of what is lived. "I believe" is validated by being rooted in life. Thus, a third question arises concerning Christian mission:

> What modes of community, thought, language, and action are appropriate for a confessional style of Christian mission to those who are captive to the limits of life today?[8]

Any situation or occasion that the Christian community enters or creates can only serve as a moment when the Holy Spirit *may* enable people to transcend the limits of life. Mission is of the essence of Christian spirituality; without mission Christian spirituality is askew. Mission, however, is the mission of God, as Hans Hoekendijck said with force.[9] Mission is carried on by the spirit of God-in-Christ. The Holy Spirit enters, opens, evokes, and empowers Christian response. In this response, Christians enter or create situations, re-present, and confess. As Christian spirituality is created by trust, so Christian mission is carried on in trust that God will use its declaration to free those held captive.

A Concluding Note

A spirituality for the long haul . . .

Is found when the mystery and clarity of God-in-Christ meets the person. This meeting takes place at those limits that stand between human beings and God.

Consists of a shift in personal identity, creativity, and character. This shift is accomplished by moving from life oriented in one of the world's peoples to life oriented in the people bonded by God-in-Christ. In this shift the graciousness of God enables the person to follow and reenact the meaning of Christ, to transcend the captivities of those limits that separate human beings from God, and to enter the true homeland of God's approaching kingdom.

Participates in a mission directed to peoples and persons. In this mission God calls us, like those in previous ages, to re-present Christ by creating limit occasions appropriate to our times wherein the Spirit may work to produce a faithful response to the One who took the form of a servant.

Notes

CHAPTER 1

1. Gustav Aulen, *Dag Hammarskjöld's White Book* (Philadelphia; Fortress Press, 1969), 97.
2. Henry P. Van Dusen, *Dag Hammarskjöld; The Statesman and His Faith* (New York: Harper & Row, 1967), 37.
3. "A Dialogue of Self and Soul" in *The Collected Poems of W, B, Yeats* (New York; Macmillan Co., 1956), 230–32.

CHAPTER 2

1. Samuel Terrien points out that this liturgy of the harvest thanksgiving probably represented the earliest stage of Israel's adaptation to agrarian culture. Nevertheless, he notes that the concern was not for a mythical fertility of the soil but for Yahweh's intervention in human history. See Terrien's *The Elusive Presence* (New York: Harper & Row, 1978), 18–19. I am indebted in many ways to this valuable book. The references to "name" and "glory" draw from the treatment of these subjects in this work.
2. Terrien, *Elusive Presence*, 40–41.
3. I owe this way of stating the problem to Paul Harrison.

CHAPTER 3

1. The use of the idea of limit here and throughout the book is indebted to David Tracy's concept of limit as developed in *Blessed Rage for Order* (New York: Seabury Press, 1975), 92–95. This leads me to acknowledge that philosophical presuppositions or ideas influence one's approach to Scripture, either deliberately or unconsciously. At the same time I have attempted to employ the limit concept in a formal way as a kind of tool for interpreting Scripture, as does Tracy (for example, his reference to Scripture as "limit language"), but without developing or relying upon a metaphysical background of the term.

2. Among the human conditions I shall describe are some that might be construed as constituting or referring to natural law or orders of creation. I do not intend any such reference. The conditions of life to which I point are not specially fixed norms, but are aspects of life at which identifiable limits are met. I suggest that these constants of life stand firmly athwart a mere relativism which maintains that the human condition is what a given age or person thinks it is, or that human existence consists of the ebb and flow of its own history. The conditions of life disclosed by Scripture stand between natural law and orders on the one hand and relativism on the other. The differentiating point is not that these conditions of life are specially fixed norms, but that they are the aspects of life in which limits are met.

CHAPTER 4

1. Walter Harrelson, "Life, Faith, and the Emergence of Tradition," in *Tradition and Theology in the Old Testament*, ed. Douglas A. Knight (Philadelphia: Fortress Press, 1977), 24.

2. Simplistic answers to the question, To whom does the "servant" refer? are obviously not helpful, but one can scarcely deny that the servant has meaning for Israel. Whether the servant is a prophecy of Christ is a different question. (See chapter 15.) Three substantial discussions of the servant songs (Isa. 42:1–4; 49:1–6; 50:4–11a; 52:13–53:12) are: Gerhard von Rad, *The Theology of Israel's Prophetic Traditions*, vol. 2 of *Old Testament Theology* (New York: Harper & Row, 1965), 250–62; Christopher R. North, *The Suffering Servant in Deutero-Isaiah*, 2nd ed., (London: Oxford University Press, 1956); *The Interpreter's Bible* (Nashville: Abingdon Press, 1956), s.v. "Introduction—Isaiah Chapters 40—66."

3. See *Theological Dictionary of the New Testament* (Grand Rapids: Wm. B. Eerdmans, 1964), s.v. "*ethnos*, OT"; "*ethnos*, NT"; "*laos*, OT"; "*laos*, NT." The word is present in all books of the Bible except the Song of Solomon, Philemon, James, and 1, 2, and 3 John. It is present in John 1:11. The passages point out that *ethnos*, which appears about one hundred times in the New Testament, is used in opposition to Jews, but that the nature of the opposition is not peoples as such but the fact that they are heathen. John's Gospel uses "world," "*kosmos*," for "heathen," not "peoples," or "*ethne*."

4. See John Bright, *A History of Israel* (Philadelphia: Westminster Press, 1959), 17ff.

5. Harrelson, "Life, Faith, and Emergence of Tradition," 25.

6. Gerhard von Rad, *The Theology of Israel's Historical Traditions*, vol. 1 of *Old Testament Theology* (New York: Harper & Row, 1965), 136. See also his *Genesis* (Philadelphia: Westminster Press, 1961), 135–41.

7. Isaiah 10:5–34; 14:4–21, 24–27 (Assyria); 14:28–32 (Philistia); 15:1—16:13 (Moab); 17:1–3 (Syria); 18:1—19:25 (Egypt); 21:11–12 and 13–17 (Arabian tribes); 23:1–18 (Phoenicia). The listing in this form has been taken

from Walter Harrelson, *Interpreting the Old Testament* (New York: Holt, Rinehart & Winston, 1964), 228–29. See also Jeremiah 46—57; Ezekiel 25—32.

8. Paul Minear, *Images of the Church in the New Testament* (Philadelphia: Westminster Press, 1959), 68.

9. Terrien, *Elusive Presence*, 124–29.

CHAPTER 5

1. Margaret Mead, *Continuities in Cultural Evolution* (New Haven, Conn. and London: Yale University Press, 1964), 38.

2. R. J. Zwi Werblowsky, "Salvation in Jerusalem," in *Concepts of Salvation, Yearbook 1976–77* (Ecumenical Institute for Advanced Religious Studies), 55.

3. Minear's *Images of the Church* lists ninety-six New Testament analogies under these headings and others.

4. In the sense indicated, for instance, in Jer. 48:42; Isa. 5:18–25.

5. See Exod. 22:21–24; Deut. 24:17–22.

6. Phil. 2:7. We shall return to this theme in chapter 15.

7. Thomas Hoyt, "To Confess Our Faith," *Occasional Papers* 9 (November 1979): 3.

CHAPTER 6

1. James Muilenberg, *The Way of Israel* (New York: Harper & Row, 1961), 49–50.

2. This theme is strong also in Ezek. 3:16–21; 18; 33.

CHAPTER 7

1. Fernand Braudel, in his two-volume work, *The Mediterranean* (New York: Harper & Row, 1973), describes how the many layers of civilization in the Mediterranean have endured over centuries, influencing the modern world as well as the successive eras and showing how very slowly change takes place.

2. The phrase is from the late Elfan Reese, one of the most experienced of those who worked internationally on behalf of post–World War II refugees. When in the fifties Henry Luce proclaimed "The Century of the Common Man," Reese, an eloquent speaker, would politely agree, and—voice rising—add: "but I suggest it is the century of the homeless man."

3. They were W. A. Visser 't Hooft of the World Council of Churches and Charles W. Ranson of the (then) International Missionary Council. I have taken slight literary license with this account. See W. A. Visser 't Hooft,

Memoirs (Philadelphia: Westminster Press, and London: SCM Press, 1973), 230–33.

CHAPTER 8

1. Erik H. Erikson, *Identity: Youth and Crisis* (New York: W. W. Norton & Co., 1968).
2. Ibid., 19.
3. Ibid.
4. Leander Keck associates "faith" as used by Paul and "trust" very closely, using the form "faith/trust" in the discussion in *Paul and His Letters* (Philadelphia: Fortress Press, 1979), 50–55.
5. I take Krister Stendahl's persuasive warning in "The Apostle Paul and the Introspective Conscience of the West" against this psychologizing tendency to mean that Paul's message has impact upon a person's identity, but that the impact, as with Paul, concerns a new calling, not a new introspectiveness. See his *Paul Among Jews and Gentiles* (Philadelphia: Fortress Press, 1976), 78–96.
6. Erikson, *Identity,* 22, 23.

CHAPTER 9

1. H. Richard Niebuhr, *Radical Monotheism and Western Culture* (New York: Harper & Brothers, 1960), 31.
2. Quoted in Winthrop S. Hudson, *Religion in America* (New York: Charles Scribner's Sons, 1965), 318.
3. Quoted in Sydney E. Ahlstrom, *A Religious History of the American People* (New Haven, Conn., and London: Yale University Press, 1972), 849.
4. The Second Inaugural Address, in *The Life and Writings of Abraham Lincoln,* ed. Philip Van Doren Stern (New York: Random House, 1940), 841–42.
5. Allan Nevins, "Lincoln in His Writings," in *Life and Writings of Lincoln,* XXIV–XXV.

CHAPTER 10

1. Walter Harrelson, *Interpreting the Old Testament* (New York: Holt, Rinehart & Winston, 1964), 157.
2. Edwyn Hoskyns, *The Fourth Gospel* (London: Faber & Faber, 1947), 137–38.
3. See *Theological Dictionary of the New Testament,* s.v. "Sin in the Old Testament," "Sin in the New Testament."
4. Gerhard von Rad, *Genesis, a Commentary,* trans. John H. Marks (Phila-

delphia: Westminster Press, 1961), 85ff.
5. Paul Ricoeur, *The Symbolism of Evil* (Boston: Beacon Press, 1969), 236.
6. Ibid., 235.
7. See *Theological Dictionary of the New Testament*, s.v. "Sin in the New Testament." This article comments that desire is not to be limited to the sensual or sexual sphere, but must be understood in a comprehensive sense as the yearning, "kindled by the Law but opposed to it, for self-assertion against the claim of God." See also Ricoeur, *Symbolism of Evil*, 142–43.
8. Patrick Henry, "A Song of Worshiping Pilgrims," *Occasional Papers* 5 (March 1978): 5.
9. To psychologize sin suggests that it may be explained wholly in psychological terms. Scripture, however, presents a theological view of sin which has penetrating psychological implications. The psychological implications of sin mean that psychological explorations and diagnoses have immediate, important bearing upon understanding the sinful self. Psychology helps to uncover the blocks, the inner tangles which so hold us that we cannot see how or what it means to worship the creature. In this sense one can read and use psychology of many varieties as an important commentary upon sin, providing one does not lose sight of the main point that sin is the state of being cut off from God because one puts the creature in place of the Creator. The intensity of this point of theological faith cannot be overemphasized. Therefore, the cure for sin is not psychological or educational self-development. Making full allowance for the contribution that both psychology and education make to penultimate human well-being, both are themselves subject to the self-worship which characterizes the race.

CHAPTER 11

1. Other passages are: Rom. 13:1ff.; 1 Cor. 2:8, 15:24–26; Eph. 1, 2:1ff.; 3:10, 6:12; Col. 1:16, 2:15; Rev. 13. Since World War II a body of scholarly work has appeared concerning the meaning of "the powers" in Scripture. The major works with which I am familiar are: Hendrik Berkhof, *Christ and the Powers*, trans. John H. Yoder (Scottdale, Pa.: Herald Press, 1977); G. B. Caird, *Principalities and Powers* (London: Oxford University Press, 1956); Oscar Cullman, *Christ and Time* (Philadelphia: Westminster Press, 1950) and *The State in the New Testament* (New York: Charles Scribner's Sons, 1956); Albert van den Heuval, *These Rebellious Powers* (New York: Friendship Press, 1965); *The Lordship of Christ Over the World and the Church* (Geneva: World Council of Churches, 1957); Paul S. Minear, *To Die and To Live* (New York: Seabury Press, 1977); Richard J. Mouw, *Politics and the Biblical Drama* (Grand Rapids: Wm. B. Eerdmans, 1976); E. Gordon Rupp, *Principalities and Powers* (London: Epworth Press, 1952); Heinrich Schlier, *Principalities and Powers in the New Testament* (New York: Herder & Herder, 1961); Ronald J.

Sider, *Evangelism, Salvation and Social Justice* (New York: Grove Books, 1977); John H. Yoder, *The Politics of Jesus* (Grand Rapids: Wm. B. Eerdmans, 1972). And to these one would want to add the seminal reference in the Barmen Declaration of the Confessing Church of Germany, Article 1: "We reject the false doctrine that the Church can and must acknowledge as a source of its proclamation, beside and in addition to this one Word of God, other events, powers, forms and truths as the revelation of God."

2. Rupp, *Principalities and Powers*, 15.

3. Berkhof, in *Christ and the Powers*, 23–24, makes a strong, clarifying point in stating that Paul demythologizes the apocalypses. The latter see the powers as heavenly angels, but Paul sees them as structures of earthly existence. "By the light of the liberation he discovers myriad forms of bondage. To give expression to the weight of such bondage he uses the current names for superterrestrial powers." See, however, note 6 below.

4. Schlier, *Principalities and Powers in the New Testament*, 16.

5. Berkhof, in *Christ and the Powers*, 12, writes: "When Hitler took the helm in Germany in 1933, the Powers of Volk, race and state took a new grip on men. . . . While studying in Berlin (1937) I myself experienced almost literally how such Powers may be 'in the air.' At the same time one had to see how they intruded as a barrier between God's word and men."

6. Berkhof's phrase (see note 3 above) is attractive, providing the word "structure" is not understood in a static sense. That meaning of structure appeared in the old concept of orders of creation by which the state, law, family, and so on were seen to be part of creation itself. The powers as structures of existence may be a clue to a certain typology of state, family, and the like, but the New Testament points to highly dynamic forces which cannot be frozen into a concept of orders.

7. Compare Rom. 13:1; 1 Pet. 2:13–17.

CHAPTER 12

1. Compare Col. 1:15–19; Heb. 1:1.

2. References for this paragraph are: Matt. 6:25ff. (see also Luke 12:22ff.); Matt. 5:43–45; Mark 4:26 (see also Matt. 13); Heb. 12:2; Matt. 8:27, Mark 4:41, Luke 8:22–25; Matt. 8:22, Luke 9:60; Matt. 10:29, Luke 12:6; Matt. 27:45, Mark 15:33, Luke 23:44; Matt. 24:29, Mark 13:24, Luke 21:25; Matt. 25:31ff.

3. Von Rad, *Genesis, a Commentary*, 58.

CHAPTER 13

1. The idea that the Old Testament stresses an angry God of judgment and the New Testament a God of love and forgiveness is far from the truth.

Throughout both Old and New Testaments, God's graciousness includes both anger and love. The phrase used at the end of this paragraph to express this is "wounded love" and is taken from *Theological Dictionary of the New Testament,* s.v. "The Wrath of Man and the Wrath of God in the New Testament." A summary Walter Eichrodt wrote concerning the Old Testament applies equally to the New. Speaking of divine punishment, Eichrodt, in *Theology of the Old Testament,* vol. 1 (Philadelphia: Westminster Press, 1961), 380, wrote that "God does this not with the strict and icy indifference of a judge, but with the pain and anger of one whose suit for a personal surrender has been rejected . . . the most severe punishment nevertheless results from a moral necessity far removed from any kind of caprice."

2. Samuel Terrien, *Elusive Presence,* 361–73.

3. For instance, personal or corporate worship of false gods, or selfish assertiveness, as in the parable of the prodigal son, etc.

4. Eschatological wrath is clearly expressed by the prophets of the eighth century, in the book of Daniel, in the Gospels, and in the writings of Paul.

5. *Theological Dictionary of the New Testament,* s.v. "The Wrath of Man and the Wrath of God in the Old Testament."

6. Stendahl, "Judgment and Mercy," in *Paul Among Jews and Gentiles,* 103.

7. Abraham Heschel, *The Prophets,* vol. 2 (New York: Harper & Row, 1971), 72.

CHAPTER 14

1. There has frequently been tension between what the church says are or should be the limits of knowledge and its actual limits. At times, the church has tried to control or suppress human inquiry. Those who resisted, often at great expense, helped greatly to establish the true distinction between artificially imposed and inherent limitations. Scripture seems to have little direct interest in this problem, save for the warrants it offers to human creativity, and its warning that the latter is not equipped to take the place of God.

2. Actually at the conclusion of Psalm 43, the two psalms originally being in all probability a single unit. Samuel Terrien, *The Psalms and Their Meaning for Today* (Indianapolis: Bobbs-Merrill, 1952), 146.

3. For references concerning the Isaiah passages, see Chapter 4, note 2. For commentary and summary of literature on John 1:1–18, see Raymond E. Brown, *The Gospel According to John 1—12* (New York: Doubleday & Co., 1976). John 1:1–14 states the servant theme less explicitly than Philippians 2:5–11, but does so implicitly. See note 4 below. For commentary and summary of literature on Phil. 2:6–11, see R. P. Martin, *Carmen Christi* (Cambridge: Cambridge University Press, 1967).

4. Oscar Cullman, *The Christology of the New Testament* (London: SCM Press, 1959).

5. As regards John 1:1–18, it is generally thought that the context of "light" is Genesis 1. There seems to be no reason, however, why "light" here may not have a double context. It may have also the context of Isaiah 42:1–9, in which the servant is given as a covenant to the people and a light to the nations, and in which this language follows a reference (v. 5) to creation. One cannot get too precise because it is the language of poetry and worship, but the double reference in Isaiah 42:1–9 to creation and light to the nations on the one hand and covenant and servant on the other suggests that John 1:1–18 may also intend the same breadth. Thus, in a different situation, Brown, in *Gospel According to John 1–12*, 60ff., accepts a double interpretation of "Lamb of God" as referring both to the servant in Isaiah and to the paschal lamb.

6. The study by Patrick Henry, *New Directions in New Testament Study* (Philadelphia: Westminster Press, 1979) contains helpful perspectives on this problem.

7. Paul "received" and "delivered." These are the essential acts implied in "tradition." Whether the tradition be living or dead is another matter. See C. H. Dodd, *The Apostolic Preaching and its Developments* (New York: Harper & Brothers, 1936) and Keck, *Paul and His Letters*, 34.

8. Is it necessary that the physical questions concerning the resurrection stand in the way of the substance? One cannot "explain" the incarnation very easily, if at all, in biophysical terms, but faith convinces one of the fact of it. I believe the same to be true of the resurrection. Paul, the earliest New Testament writer, does not speak of the manner of the resurrection in the above sense, thus indirectly testifying that the fact of it to his experience supersedes the details of its circumstances.

9. A cogent article on this point is Nils Dahl, "The Neglected Factor in New Testament Theology," *Reflection* (November 1975.)

10. H. Richard Niebuhr, *The Kingdom of God in America* (New York: Harper & Row, 1937), 193.

CHAPTER 15

1. This personal, interior, transforming experience was invited by Jesus in Matt. 10:38; Mark 8:34; Luke 14:27; John 3:17–21; and in the account presented by Acts, which in large part demonstrates the promise in Acts 1:8.

2. Berkhof, in *Christ and the Powers*, 42, prefers "disarmed" to the RSV "destroyed" on the grounds that the Greek *katargein* means "to make ineffective," "to disconnect."

3. Ibid., 49.

4. In addition to John 1:ff.; Eph. 1; Col. 1:16; Heb. 1:2. Of Paul's thought, Leander Keck, in *Paul and His Letters*, 76, writes: "Being rooted in Judaism and its Scripture, Paul assumed that God is the Creator. . . . Whereas the deutero-Pauline letters to the Colossians and Ephesians emphasize the relation of the pre-existent Son of God to Creation . . . , the undisputed letters

virtually ignore this. However, given Paul's appropriation of Jewish wisdom theology, and given the occasional nature of the letters as well, one should not infer that this theme was of no interest to Paul."

5. From the hymn "New Every Morning" by John Keble.

CHAPTER 16

1. This is the theme of Samuel Terrien's *Elusive Presence*. See the book's preface, xxvii–xxviii.

2. "For all" appears in different expressions and contexts. See, for example, Matt. 26:28; Mark 14:24; Luke 22:19–20; John 1:9, 6:51, 15:13; 1 Cor. 11:24, 15:3; 2 Cor. 5:14; Heb. 7:27; 1 Pet. 3:18. See also Joachim Jeremias, *The Central Message of the New Testament*, (New York: Charles Scribner's Sons, 1965), 31–50.

3. It lies beyond our scope to discuss *how* God's presence is already among all the world's peoples. The manner of testimony here envisaged implies, as regards other religions, a steadfast testimony coupled with dialogue and not coercive, for instance, in the form of claiming superiority. One cannot testify without believing that one's testimony is true. My testimony or the church's testimony to the truth in the Servant and concerning the Servant is denied by any show of pride. That there has been so much pride in the church's preaching of the truth is one of its greatest shames.

4. Three of Jesus' severe warnings, for instance, seem to be especially marked by care for persons: Matt. 25:1–13; Mark 13:1–37; Luke 12:35–46.

5. Von Rad, *Theology of the Old Testament*, 1:231. Also *Theological Dictionary of the New Testament*, s.v. *"parakleseo," "paraklesis."*

6. We noted in chapter 5 the Old Testament conviction that a people must give loyalty to God. If a people, or a minority of the people, does not do that, is the church justified in warning that people about its lack of loyalty to God? Does that not force the church's belief upon the people? I believe that the church may legitimately warn a nation as to its loyalties, no matter what the particular minority/majority situation of the church may be, but with the provisos that the warning is issued not to protect the church's narrow interests, but with authentic care for the nation or the people; and provided that the people is not manipulated by legislation or by other factors into complying with the church's warning.

7. Hosea 1:2, which states the prophetic attack upon Israel's perversion of the covenant. See also Acts 5:1–11.

8. The end of the centuries-long period of Christendom produced varied responses: the Barmen Declaration (of the Confessing Church in Germany) and its insistence upon the integrity of the church and ensuing resistance to Hitler; the "steadfast, patient endurance" of churches under other totalitarian regimes; the impulse, especially after the demise of colonialism, toward par-

ticipation in nation building; liberation movements and theology of varied accents. White Christians and churches in the United States have largely been spectators of these developments and participants in the debates by choice, not by necessity, because the U.S. form of Christendom was largely undisturbed—indeed, reinforced and made prosperous—by World War II. With fissures opening in the sixties, debate has just begun in the United States, but it seems to be carried on largely by a small number of the white majority in the churches. The black church and Christians in other racial groups participated only minimally in U.S. Christendom and lived parallel to but outside the witness of the white majority.

9. See Joseph M. Shaw et al., eds., *Readings in Humanism* (Minneapolis: Augsburg Publishing House, 1982).

10. This discussion took place at the Institute for Ecumenical and Cultural Research, Collegeville, Minnesota, in July 1980 and 1981.

11. Stress here is upon the attitude. For example, the impact of Jesus' parables is frequently to raise a question with the hearer.

12. This discussion took place at the Institute for Ecumenical and Cultural Research, Collegeville, Minnesota, in July 1979.

13. And also in other social conditions. I should argue that in a situation where revolution is finally necessary, negotiation should nevertheless be the objective.

CHAPTER 17

1. See the seven-volume work by Kenneth Scott Latourette, *A History of the Expansion of Christianity* (New York: Harper & Brothers, 1937–45).

2. Thomas F. Stransky, CSP and Gerald H. Anderson, *Mission Trends No. 3*, (Ramsey, N.J.: Paulist Press and Grand Rapids: Wm. B. Eerdmans, 1976), 1, 6.

3. For two reflections on this point, see James B. Conant, *Modern Science and Modern Man* (Garden City, N.Y.: Doubleday & Co., 1953); and L. V. Berkner, *The Scientific Age* (New Haven, Conn.: Yale University Press, 1964).

4. Muilenberg, *The Way of Israel*, 45.

5. Matthew 13:31; Mark 4:30–32; Luke 13:18–19—and other parables of seed. Also, John 3:3ff.; 1 John 3:19; 1 Pet. 1:3, 23; John 13:20; Col. 1:13; Rom. 5:10–11; 2 Cor. 5:16ff.; Col. 1:20; Rom. 8:19ff.; Gal. 6:15.

6. The analogy may be developed in two stages. First, as law made sin come alive for Paul, so peoplehood gives sin its particular form and shape for people generally. This stage of an analogy rests upon the fact that "law" meant the commandments or revealed will of God for ancient Israel, and this was the basis of Israel's peoplehood. The important reference in Rom. 2:13ff. to those of the Gentiles (peoples) who do the law without the law, by conscience, gives a further basis to this part of the analogy. The second stage of the analogy

proceeds from sin to all other limits, on the ground that sin affects them all and that all, like sin, are limits. Peoplehood, however, is overarching, as the limit which colors or gives shape to, all others.

7. See chapter 9, "The Re-presentative Limit-Language of Christology," in Tracy's *Blessed Rage for Order*. I neither affirm nor criticize the content of Tracy's re-presentation, but stress the urgent appropriateness of the term itself.

8. The sequence here is deliberate so as to engage anything and everything done; for example, worship requires thought, language, and action, and so on.

9. See chapters 1 and 2 of J. C. Hoekendijk's *The Church Inside Out* (Philadelphia: Westminster Press, 1964).